WHISPERING SMITH

WHISPERING SMITH
HIS LIFE AND MISADVENTURES

ALLEN P. BRISTOW

SANTA FE

© 2007 by Allen P. Bristow. All Rights Reserved.
No part of this book may be reproduced in any form or by any electronic or mechanical means including information storage and retrieval systems without permission in writing from the publisher, except by a reviewer who may quote brief passages in a review.

Sunstone books may be purchased for educational, business, or sales promotional use. For information please write:
Special Markets Department, Sunstone Press,
P.O. Box 2321, Santa Fe, New Mexico 87504-2321.

Library of Congress Cataloging-in-Publication Data

Bristow, Allen P.
  Whispering Smith : his life and misadventures / by Allen P. Bristow.
     p. cm.
  Includes bibliographical references and index.
  ISBN 978-0-86534-551-5 (softcover : alk. paper)
   1. Smith, Whispering, d. 1914. 2. Outlaws--West (U.S.)--Biography.
3. Railroad police--West (U.S.)--Biography. 4. Detectives--West
(U.S.)--Biography. 5. Detectives--Louisiana--New Orleans--Biography.
6. Adventure and adventurers--West (U.S.)--Biography. 7. Frontier
and pioneer life--West (U.S.) 8. West (U.S.)--History--1860-1890--
Biography. 9. New Orleans (La.)--Biography. I. Title.

F594.S666B75 2007
978'.02092--dc22
[B]
                              2007018572

WWW.SUNSTONEPRESS.COM
SUNSTONE PRESS / POST OFFICE BOX 2321 / SANTA FE, NM 87504-2321 /USA
(505) 988-4418 / ORDERS ONLY (800) 243-5644 / FAX (505) 988-1025

TO FRED AND GINGER

CONTENTS

PREFACE / 9

ACKNOWLEDGEMENTS / 11

1 / HOLLYWOOD VERSUS HISTORY / 13

2 / THE EARLY YEARS / 17

3 / LOUISIANA / 29

4 / NEBRASKA / 46

5 / NEW MEXICO / 75

6 / WYOMING / 85

7 / UTAH / 97

8 / COLORADO / 124

9 / END OF THE TRAIL / 137

ADDENDUM / 147

NOTES / 156

BIBLIOGRAPHY / 166

INDEX / 171

PREFACE

A MYRIAD OF DIFFICULTIES were encountered when Whispering Smith's life history was explored. His surname was a constant impediment. Smith is the most prevalent name in the United States, followed by Johnson and Williams. The commonality of his given name, James, in combination with his surname added hundreds of hours to searches of indexes, genealogical and public records. Great caution was required to insure that the Smith found was actually "Whispering Smith" and in some cases a decision was necessarily based on the preponderance of evidence.

Another difficulty was the nature of Smith's career. Many periods of his life were spent in activities of a sub-rosa nature and employers insured that his adventures received little publicity. Exceptions occurred when court appearances, lawsuits and newspaper articles brought him to public attention. Smith's personality was still another factor that obscures his past. He was secretive by nature, preferred seclusion, had few friends and no family.

When gaps fell between Smith's known activities the technique of juxtaposing his movements with other accounts of related history and events was employed. It was the task of this biographer to fill such gaps with the best estimate possible based on Whispering Smith's known personality, predilections, temperament and life style. It is hoped that future revelations may clarify the obscure portions of his life.

ACKNOWLEDGEMENTS

MANY RESEARCHERS, HISTORIans and archivists contributed to the search for Whispering Smith's past and without their help this work would not have been possible. They include Rob Rybolt for his Nebraska lore, Trish Surles, Christopher Smithson and Glovenea Snead for Maryland genealogy, Carolyn Billups for Civil War veteran research, Terry Foenander for Mississippi Naval Squadron history, Heidi Myers (U. S. Naval Historical Center) for Civil War naval history, Jean Nathan and John Hopkins for Mississippi River duels, Shugana Campbell (Amistad Center) for Freedmen's Bureau research, Mary N. White for New Orleans and Metropolitan Police information, William Kratville (Union Pacific Railway Historian) for Nebraska railroad lore, Murray L. Carroll for Wyoming Stock Growers Association correspondence, Sue Ann Martell for Castle Gate history and Candice Polk for Denver County Jail records.

1

HOLLYWOOD VERSUS HISTORY

THE BEST-SELLING NOVEL OF 1906 was titled *Whispering Smith* and was written by Frank H. Spearman following a visit to Cheyenne, Wyoming. His purpose was to consult with two men that were considered to be leading authorities on railroad policing. They were Union Pacific Special Agent Timothy T. Keliher and U. S. Deputy Marshal Joe LeFors.[1] They sat for hours in the bar of the Inter-Ocean Hotel, the principal watering hole in Cheyenne. Spearman sought to learn the techniques of railroad policing and the problems affecting officers that protected the rails in the west.

Spearman, never a railroader himself, became familiar with the romance of the rails through his contacts with the

Union Pacific Railway while a Nebraska banker. He authored several books with railroad plots prior to the Cheyenne trip and one, *The Strategy of Great Railroads*, was adopted as a textbook at Yale University in 1904. As a young man he was involved in mid-western commerce and heard of a man called Whispering Smith. The name made a lasting impression on his memory and when he began to write fiction he used it in a short story. LeFors and Keliher must have mentioned a man they had known called Whispering Smith, thus reinforcing Spearman's fascination with the name. His involvement with Keliher and LeFors inspired a new novel centering on a railroad detective they had described and the character was to be called Whispering Smith.[2]

There actually was a Union Pacific Railway detective that served in the Nebraska and Wyoming area during the late 1870s and who came to be known as Whispering Smith. His true name was James L. Smith. While Spearman created his heroic character as a fictional composite of Keliher and LeFors, he could not resist the appealing nature of James L. Smith's nickname. It is unknown if Spearman ever met Smith in person, corresponded with him or if Smith was ever aware of the novel.

In a 1916 novel, *Nan of Music Mountain*, Spearman wove an exciting story of stage line robbery. This long and wordy novel was paced much like *Whispering Smith* and that fictional railroad detective was frequently included in the dialogue. Although James L. Smith died two years prior to publication of this second novel one wonders if he was aware of Spearman's continued fascination with his nickname. The popularity of Smith's sobriquet was predictable. The public of that period was greatly attracted to the colorful names linked with characters of the old west. Celebrated examples include Wild Bill, Buffalo Bill, Bronco Billy, Black Bart, Billy the Kid, and Calamity Jane.

    Hollywood pounced on Spearman's catchy title plus the popularity of his 1906 novel and repeatedly obtained filming rights.[3] With each new motion picture the story line strayed farther from the plot of Spearman's novel. Hollywood filmmakers, in order to maximize the appeal of the western genre, created an entire mythology of inaccurate impressions with respect to language, accents, equipment, apparel, demeanor and grooming. Their fictionalization included heroic gunfighters, quick-draw shootouts, grunting Indians, quirky side-kicks, trick riding cowboys and defense of vulnerable womanhood. This fanciful coloration was applied to the Whispering Smith films, much to the distortion of history.[4]

    In Spearman's 1906 novel Whispering Smith investigates the deliberate wrecking of trains by thieving salvage crews. He identifies an old friend as the principal scoundrel after the plot is delayed by romantic interludes. In a final chase the villain is killed by Smith's sidekick. Smith is then hospitalized with an illness but manages to win his true love. Spearman's book was illustrated by N. C. Wyeth using the proper apparel of the era. The film versions of the novel are progressively rewritten to change the plot and lose most of the detail that Spearman originally included on railroad policing, use of informants and pay-offs made to troublemakers.[5]

In 1948 the most popular film version featured Alan Ladd in his first color appearance. Ladd's characterization of Whispering Smith portrayed a mild-mannered, two-gun railroad detective whose quiet voice and polite demeanor triumphs over evil. Ladd appears as a slightly built and clean-shaven hero dressed in Hollywood's version of cowboy attire complete with a Buscadero gun belt and a pair of pearl handled Colt Peacemaker revolvers. This image was incorrect in every detail.

The common thread woven through the novel and the films cast Whispering Smith as an honest, moral man who took no advantage in a fight and whose courage never failed. Were Spearman and Hollywood guilty of a mischaracterization? Was the real Whispering Smith actually a cold-blooded killer, frustrated duelist, devious plotter and pugnacious braggart? These questions can best be answered by an examination of his life.

2

THE EARLY YEARS

TWO MEN LOUNGED UNCOMfortably in the front room of a shabby house on New Orleans' Feret Street near the corner of Jackson just before dawn on Sunday, May 24, 1874. One studied the street through a window too long unwashed. The other dozed fitfully on a sofa in the corner. They were Metropolitan Police detectives.

The sleeper was Thomas Devereaux. Long sideburns accentuated his swarthy complexion and a pork-pie hat was angled so the brim shielded his eyes from the gleam cast by the gas light outside the window. His legs were drawn up and wedged against the back of the sofa to keep the two shotguns stored there from falling. That pair of long double-barreled weapons would have looked more at home in a duck blind instead of a street-level room in this vice-ridden neighborhood.

The watcher was James L. Smith. His black eyes burned with intensity as he watched the last of the street prostitutes lead her customer toward an alley. A prominent Roman nose that perched over a drooping mustache commanded Smith's face. He nervously stroked his Imperial goatee and focused on a man that appeared in the doorway across the street. Smith's thin, tightly clamped lips parted just enough for a whisper to his partner. "Tom! Come look. Is that him?"

"It's Munson Alexander all right!" Devereaux responded as he clapped Smith on the back. "Let's get into the street. If he walks out we'll get him good this time!"

The pair stepped outside and stood in the shadow of the balcony. They cast a threatening appearance. Both held their shotguns at the ready. Round button-like badges of the Metropolitan Police were pinned to the lapels of their sack suits and, except for their faces and Smith's hat, a casual observer would have been unable to tell them apart. Smith's broad-brimmed fedora was a distinctive white and was his trademark on the streets of New Orleans.

Munson Alexander, their quarry, limped into Feret Street and turned toward the corner of Jackson. The left leg of his trousers was bloodstained and his gait wobbled as he favored it. The detectives called for him to halt. Alexander twisted to see who was behind him and then attempted to run. Within a few steps he stopped, turned and drew a revolver. Smith fired one shotgun barrel over Alexander's head but Devereaux discharged both barrels directly at him. Munson Alexander fell mortally wounded on the cobblestone street. At least that's the version that Smith claimed in his report of the encounter upon which this scenario is based.[6]

This shooting incident involving the man who was to become Whispering Smith, and the turmoil that followed, well predicted the next forty years of his adventurous career.

Documentation is lacking for much of the first third of James L. Smith's life. One clue from census listings indicates that he was probably born about January of 1838.[7] A second clue is found on his 1873 marriage registration. This document, written by a clerk, indicated that his father was James Smith, his mother was Lydia Perry and confirmed that he was born in Maryland.[8] The search for the origin of Whispering Smith was based on this meager information.

At once the paucity of genealogical records for Maryland in the early nineteenth century became an impediment. Civil registration of births did not begin until 1875 at Baltimore and 1898 in the balance of the state. Various churches kept some vital records but their survival and availability is limited. Federal census records are intact from 1790 but no mid-decade state enumerations were taken. County clerks began to record marriage licenses as early as 1777 and those records do provide a possible theory as to the origin of James L. Smith.

While the Maryland marriage indexes had many entries for a James Smith, there was but one for a Lydia Perry. On a license issued in Anne Arundel County on January 5, 1825, she was listed as the bride and one Joseph Smith was shown as the groom.[9] The discrepancy between Joseph and James as the name of James L. Smith's father may have several explanations. The 1873 New Orleans marriage document was written by a Parish Recorder and based on the verbal information provided to him by the participants. There may have been a great deal of hilarity, confusion and joyful intoxication at the time as well as a possible English-French language complication.

Anne Arundel County was bordered on the north by the city of Baltimore and the Chesapeake Bay to the east. In the early nineteenth century farming and fishing supported its population. A Joseph Smith is listed in the 1840 U. S. Census as residing in southern Anne Arundel County and his family fits a likely profile.[10]

> Male 40-50...1, Probably Joseph Smith, born 1793 and 32 years old at the time of his marriage in 1825.
>
> Female 30-40...1, Probably Lydia Smith (Perry) born in 1805 and 20 years old at the time of her marriage in 1825.
>
> Female 15-20...1, Probably Lydia born in 1825 in first year of the marriage.
>
> Male 10-15...Unknown son.
>
> Male 5-10...Unknown son.
>
> Female under 5...Unknown daughter.
>
> Male under 5...Probably James L. Smith, born in 1838 and age 2 at time of the census.

If this last listed male is James L. Smith his chronological placement among the sons of Joseph Smith may indicate that he was named after one of the father's brothers. Naming practices of that era often awarded the given name of an uncle to third and later born sons.

Joseph Smith's family is not found in the 1850 census but emerges again in 1860.

Living in Baltimore's First Ward were Joseph at age sixty-seven and Lydia at age fifty-five. No children were still with them but there were three boarders.[11] In 1870 Lydia was living in Baltimore's Thirteenth Ward at age sixty-five. With her was Lydia, likely the oldest daughter and first born among the children.[12] Joseph apparently died prior to 1870 but no probate record can be found.

Left unanswered is the whereabouts of James L. Smith, probably the youngest in the family. One possibility is that he was given to be raised by an uncle, perhaps his namesake, James H. Smith, a carpenter residing in Wilmington, Delaware. The 1850 census displays that family with three other children aged five, three and one.[13] The last listed is James Smith, born in Maryland and of fourteen years. James H. Smith and his wife, Eveline, were born in Maryland but the three youngest children were born in Delaware. The non-sequential manner in which young James was listed indicates that he may not have been a birth child of that couple. The plausible foster father relationship with James H. Smith may also explain the confusion of names on Whispering Smith's wedding document.

Speculation on the status of this young James Smith involves the possibility that James H. Smith was a younger brother of Joseph Smith whose family may have grown too large for his income. Perhaps the youngest son was sent to live with his uncle. The variance in age, listed as fourteen when it should have been twelve, may be due to the foster parents ignorance or indifference when giving information to the census enumerator. It may also have been an attempt to remove the lad from classification as an infant so that he might be apprenticed to a trade. Fourteen was the traditional age to enter an apprenticeship and also the age to have completed grammar school. Some apprentices received room and board from their employer and this may also have been the reason for the foster parents to add two years to his age.

Wilmington had become a shipbuilding center on the Atlantic coast in that era. The shipyards produced ocean-going steamships and smaller craft suitable for river commerce. The demand for workers skilled in the required trades was intense and apprenticeship opportunities in boiler-making, calking, carpentry and the foundry arts were frequent.

This estimate of Whispering Smith's early years is obviously speculation based on likely relationships but it is the most logical explanation yet found. Nothing as confident is available for the late teen years and his life remains undocumented until a segment of his obituary places him in the Mississippi River area just prior to the War of the Rebellion.

The American Civil War brought over two-million men to Union military service and it was a youthful conflict. Men aged no more that twenty constituted the majority in uniform. Conscription insured that few escaped service. James L. Smith was twenty-three when hostilities began and it is probable that he participated, given his violent and combative history in the post-bellum period. Regrettably, a search of military records at the National Archives and other sources give no strong documentation although some clues relating to Smith's service were available.

The strongest reference to his military history was

given by Bronson in his book, *The Red Blooded Heroes of the Frontier*, where he wrote, "...he had served with great credit as a captain of artillery in the Union Army."[14] Rob Rybolt, a Nebraska history enthusiast that became interested in Smith theorized that he was a captain in the Third Ohio Artillery or a captain of Maryland cavalry but gave no documentation. Military service and pension records do not substantiate either suggestion.[15]

One unlikely clue to Confederate service exists in a veteran's survey taken in 1890 at Emery County, Utah. One James L. Smith was listed as a Confederate scout from July1861, to January, 1862, but other information required on the form is missing. Whispering Smith was in Utah in 1890 but nothing further can be found indicating he was the same person as this veteran. On the possibility that this veteran could have been mistakenly labeled as a Confederate soldier the Union records for scouts and spies were also searched but to no avail.

The phrase "don't remember" was entered for this veteran's rank and organization. This data was, however, listed for every other veteran on the schedule. Rare is the soldier that would forget such information, thus the entire listing lacks credibility.

The later appointment of James L. Smith as a plantation inspector for the Freedmen's Bureau in Louisiana and as a New Orleans Metropolitan detective does, however, strongly indicate that he was a Union veteran and had prior service in that geographic area. Both of these organizations had an official mandate to employ former Union servicemen.

The reason that his army records are elusive may be because he was in the Union Navy! This theory originates from a portion of Smith's obituary that claims he fought a duel with one Larry Boyle, an Australian gambler, on a Mississippi riverboat named the *Belle of Memphis* just before the Civil War.[16] This would place him in the Mississippi or Ohio River area as a riverboat passenger or crew member near the start of hostilities. Among a plethora of Lawrence Boyle listings there is but one "Larry Boyle" in the 1860 U. S. Census and he was employed in river commerce at Cincinnati.[17] His birthplace is given as Ireland but there was an Irish immigration flow to the United States through Australia.

The *Belle of Memphis*, often referred to as just the *Memphis*, was built in 1860 at Jeffersonville, Indiana, just across the Ohio River from Louisville, Kentucky. She was owned by the Anchor Lines Company, used St. Louis, Missouri, as home port and served a route from Cincinnati to Memphis and New Orleans.[18] While no record is found of the duel or a connection between the *Belle of Memphis* and Smith or Boyle, Smith's known bellicosity and his obituary enhance the probability of the event. Dueling had become illegal in many of the states bordering the Mississippi and Ohio Rivers and most of the encounters never found their way into the press, thus are unrecorded.[19] The incident does, however, tie Smith to river commerce and may place him in the vicinity of Ohio and Illinois.

Cairo, Illinois, became the center for Union Navy activity at the beginning of the Civil War. The Mississippi Squadron was formed there and on October 8, 1862, James L. Smith was appointed Acting Second Engineer on the ironclad U.S.S. *Baron DeKalb*. His rank was equivalent to that of a Navy Lieutenant indicating that he had some higher education or training. He was soon promoted to Acting First Engineer and was listed as a citizen of Indiana which may further link him to the *Belle of Memphis* as she was built in that state.[20]

The date of Smith's appointment was well after the three months service as a scout claimed by the James L. Smith in the 1890 veterans survey. Thus it is possible that, if both these men were the same person, he functioned as a scout or spy somewhere in the Mississippi River system before becoming a Union naval engineer.

How would Smith have become qualified as a steam engineer on a river boat? The records of some other volunteer engineers in the Mississippi Squadron show they had previous experience with railroads or commercial steam boats. Perhaps Smith entered the westward migration from Maryland by employment with the Baltimore & Ohio Railroad. This may have provided steam engine experience and perhaps he was also involved in engineering on the *Belle of Memphis* prior to the war. It is also possible that as a youth Smith entered a boilermaker or coopers apprenticeship at the seaport of Wilmington, Delaware.

The U.S.S. *Baron DeKalb* was assigned to Mississippi Squadron Number One and she was closely involved in the riverine warfare so important to Union strategy. The squadron's mission was to seize control of the Mississippi River and its major tributaries in support of army campaigns. The *Baron DeKalb* fought in nearly every battle along the river system including Fort Donelson, Fort Henry, Island Number Ten, Fort Pillow, Memphis and Vicksburg. She was sunk by a mine at the mouth of the Yazoo River on July 13, 1863.[21]

Engineer Smith must have been transferred to the U.S.S. *Rattler* at that point. The Confederacy, now deprived of its primary defenses in the region, resorted to guerrilla warfare along the river systems. The *Rattler* was involved in counter-insurgency operations and employed landing parties to disrupt enemy activities, destroy installations and seize vessels.

One task of the Mississippi Squadron was to help recently freed slaves that were officially called "contrabands." Landing parties along the rivers brought numbers of contrabands back aboard the ironclad vessels. Most were transported to safety but some were enlisted in the U. S. Navy and were given work assignments appropriate to their skills. The engine rooms of the ironclad steamships received many of these former slaves.

Over 2,000 contrabands served on vessels in the Mississippi Squadron. They provided valuable service but required extensive supervision and training. In a sense, the effort was a forerunner of the Freedmen's Bureau that was created in the post-bellum era and perhaps this experience was related to Smith's later employment with that organization in Louisiana.

No specific instances of Smith's service on the *Rattler* can be found but he did send off a sharp complaint to Rear Admiral David D. Porter at Cairo on March 29, 1864. He had the temerity to challenge regulations that required him, as First Assistant Engineer on the U.S.S. *Rattler*, to act in the capacity of a watch officer.[22] The result of his complaint is not known but this type of brusk missive was typical of Whispering Smith, particularly in his later career with the Wyoming Stock Growers Association.

James L. Smith resigned his commission effective May 31, 1864, having served not quite two years. He cited illness although no records can be found to substantiate his medical condition. Perhaps his position had become untenable following his intemperate letter to the Admiral and discharge was his only option. Perhaps it was a wise decision because the *Rattler* was sunk on December 30, 1864.

Was this the man who later became known as Whispering Smith? He was in the correct area at the appropriate time to have enlisted at Cairo and may have had prior steamship experience. Further, his service in the southern sector of the riverine campaign would have placed him close to his Louisiana involvements following the war.[23]

3

LOUISIANA

FOG, DRIFTING IN FROM THE Mississippi River cast a diffused glow around the torches in the plantation's stable yard. A solitary figure stepped from the shadow of the carriage house as a detail of Union cavalrymen trotted past the smokehouse to halt in front of him. The sergeant in charge dismounted and approached the taller man, an official of obvious command presence. He gave a sloppy salute and said, "We got here quick as we could. Don't dare run the horses at night in this fog. To hear the Provost Marshal tell it, no need to hurry anyway…he ain't gonna go nowhere."

The official, a plantation inspector with the Freedmen's Bureau, agreed and pointed toward a barn at the edge of the stable yard. "You'll find him hanging from the beam over the barn door. Get him cut down. Find a wagon and get him back to your barracks. Don't let any of the darkies see the body...they get any more scared and they'll all run away." Both men walked to the barn and looked up at the body hung there. The small negro was naked and blood dripped from a severe whipping. He was suspended by a rope that formed a noose around his neck and was threaded through a block and tackle attached to the beam.

"Second one this month," remarked the sergeant.

"The White League did it for sure. They want to scare the blacks into working on the owner's terms. The overseer himself reported this to the bureau. We think he wanted to advertise it to all the ex-slaves working here. Otherwise they'd just throw the body in the river the way they used to do. Nothing we can do about it...just get him out of here!"

Was the plantation inspector in this scenario the man who was later to become Whispering Smith? This fictional incident was typical of the times in Louisiana and he might well have been involved in similar events as James L. Smith was apparently a plantation inspector there from 1865 to 1868.

By the end of the Civil War approximately four-million slaves had been freed. They became a severe problem in the government's reconstruction efforts. The War Department was charged with creating an agency to sustain the former slaves and protect their rights. It was commonly called the Freedmen's Bureau. Congress failed to sufficiently fund the new organization and U. S. Army commanders were forced to assign detached military personnel to staff required positions. Former Union veterans were universally employed as replacements when funds became available.

The surviving southern agricultural interests hired former slaves as farm workers. Freedmen's Bureau agents oversaw labor contracts in an effort to insure fairness. Planters were coerced by agents in many cases and the opportunities for graft were endless, particularly among Negrophobic military officers that had little interest in the goals of the bureau. Planter resistance and public opinion was reflected by southern legislatures and they enacted a variety of laws to control former slaves. These codes were harsh and forced blacks into working conditions similar to their previous slavery.[24]

The extent of violence directed against former slaves in Louisiana is reflected by a report issued in the second year of the Freedmen's Bureau operations. It was estimated that the aggregate number of murders would be more than doubled had all the cases been reported to the plantation inspectors. The total for 1866 indicates the extent of the violence.

Freedmen killed by whites: 70
Freedmen killed in addition during riots: 10
Freedmen killed, perpetrators unknown: 6
Freedmen severely wounded: 210
Freedmen wounded in addition at riots: 20
Freedmen killed by freedmen: 2
Whites killed by Freedmen: 1[25]

The Freedmen's Bureau had authority to administer justice where blacks were concerned, investigate crimes, levy fines up to $1,000 and extend military protection to those who were denied rights by local authorities. Intervention by its agents often created violent encounters in an environment already sensitized by the presence of occupation troops. Many agents were involved in fraudulent practices and this furthered public distrust but today that negative aspect is largely ignored and history views the bureau as a relief agency that failed to achieve significant advances for former slaves.[26]

The Plantation Department was created by the bureau in July, 1865. Captain Frank Bagley was assigned as its supervisor and seven inspectors were appointed to travel throughout Louisiana for the protection of former slaves employed in agriculture. Their records indicate that James L. Smith was one of these plantation inspectors as of September, 1865.[27] His salary was set at $100 per month, an amount equivalent to the salary of a U. S. Navy Lieutenant. Smith's activities as a plantation inspector are unknown but the inspectors were involved in a wide range of duties. They documented crimes against former slaves, brought legal action against their persecutors and often were in direct confrontation with hostile white elements. The spirit of this protective mission was later carried into the duties of the New Orleans Metropolitan Police and Smith would have brought valuable experience to that organization.

Was this man Whispering Smith? There seem to be no personnel records that document the identity of plantation inspectors except by name but the duties executed would fit closely with Smith's later career with the New Orleans Metropolitan Police and his following law enforcement involvements. His riverine experiences would have familiarized him with the plantation environment along the lower Mississippi River and the supervision of freed slaves, thus he would have been well qualified for appointment as a plantation inspector. The termination of the Freedmen's Bureau in 1868 coordinates with the beginning of the Metropolitan Police and Smith's rapid advancement there would indicate prior administrative or investigative experience.

Whispering Smith's obituary claimed, among other attainments, that he had once been the Chief of Detectives at New Orleans.[28] Perhaps this information was volunteered to reporters by Smith during the 1905 Masterson interviews nine years prior to his death and used by the obituary editor. Perhaps it was furnished to the newspaper by acquaintances who had known him late in life when old age and braggadocio may have colored his anecdotes. There is no evidence that Smith was ever more than a detective, special officer and warden while a member of the New Orleans Metropolitan Police.

Several listings are found for James L. Smith in New Orleans City Directories. The earliest, in 1873, records him as, "James L. Smith, Detective, Metropolitan Police, r, 157 Carondelet."[29]

The Metropolitan Police force was created by the Louisiana state government as a result of conflict between the pro-Confederate New Orleans city government and the pro-Union Republican governor following the Civil War. The primary mission of this new police organization was to restore post-bellum order in greater New Orleans, provide protection for freed slaves, insure honest elections and improve social services. Under Republican control the Metropolitan Police terminated most members that had Confederate or Democratic sympathies and focused on replacing them with those that had recently served in the Union forces. James L. Smith probably entered into Metropolitan Police service in 1868 when the Freedmen's Bureau was dissolved.

The old city of New Orleans presented a challenging setting for the newly formed police service. Its multi-cultural population evolved from early French settlers and slave traders, followed by the Spanish and Acadians, A second French occupation established the

Napoleonic Code that persisted after the United States acquired the Louisiana area. The city exceeded 100,000 in population by 1840 and became the South's largest slave trading market. Although Louisiana was the sixth state to secede, the city voted three-to-one to remain in the Union. Under Confederate control at the beginning of the war it soon fell to Union forces. It was, as the war ended, a city divided between pro-Confederate and pro-Union groups and overrun by shelter-seeking former slaves from the plantations. These conditions presented a turbulent policing environment.

The Metropolitan Police grew rapidly from its inception in 1868. By 1870 it consisted of 679 members that were distributed among nine precincts and six sub-stations. A captain commanded each precinct. It should be noted that Smith, in his rank as a detective, earned a salary roughly equivalent to that of a captain. It was a tradition that detectives or special officers served directly under the Chief of Police where they enjoyed great opportunities to exercise influence and participate in graft.[30]

Police records of this period are all but non-existent. An attempt to document Smith's activities found little in official records but various directories, court transcripts and newspaper articles provided limited information. One of the earliest documents found for Smith was his marriage license obtained on March 11, 1872, at New Orleans. The marriage was delayed until February 14, 1873. On that date the Reverend Father J. J. Duffo of the Church of

Immaculate Conception at 120 Baronne Street conducted the wedding of James L. Smith, age thirty-five, and Anna Mannion, age twenty. James was listed as a native of Maryland and Anna as born in Ireland.[31]

Additional information in the document indicated that Smith's parents were James Smith and Lydia Perry. Anna's parents were Jarred Mannion and Catherine Rodreques. One witness was Thomas Devereaux, also a member of the Metropolitan Police. This officer, whose stormy career merits later mention, was apparently Smith's close friend.

In the year of Smith's marriage the same New Orleans street directory lists Thomas Devereaux at the Superintendents Office, Metropolitan Police, 364 Poydras. Mrs. Catherine Rodreques Mannion was living at 111 Marais and it is thought that she was Anna Mannion's mother. Smith's address on Carondelet was just seven blocks south of Catherine Mannion's residence, one block south of the Immaculate Conception Church and about six blocks north of the Metropolitan Police Headquarters where he was probably assigned.

That the wedding took place a year after the license was obtained indicates an acceptable engagement period for that era and that the Mannion family held to traditional values. The yearlong delay may also have been related to Anna's widowhood and the period of mourning required by the society in which they lived. In any event, indications are that it was a serious relationship and the wedding on Saint Valentines Day is the only romantic episode found in Whispering Smith's life. The wedding would have taken place in close proximity to the Mardi Gras celebration and the intoxicating exuberance of these events may have contributed to any inaccuracies in the various marriage records.

Sadly, James L. Smith divorced Anna on November 9, 1885, at Sidney, Nebraska. He charged that she was willfully absent from him for over two years.[32] This divorce document confirms that the James L. Smith who was a railroad and stock detective in Nebraska and Wyoming was the former New Orleans detective. It also establishes that his middle name was Louis. Anna returned to New Orleans and later married one Frank L. Chanson, then died there on June 6, 1906, at the age of fifty-three. Catherine Mannion, Anna's mother, died in New Orleans on March 20, 1902, at the age of eighty-nine.[33]

Within a year of his New Orleans marriage Smith was promoted to a still more influential position. The Metropolitan Police maintained an extensive compound to lodge the large number of vagrants, homeless and destitute persons created by the post-war depression and freeing of the slaves. The 1874 street directory lists Smith as Warden of this City Work House where he resided, presumably with his bride.[34]

Such a position lent itself to financial advantage in the purchase and distribution of food, clothing and the administration of outside labor contracts. Smith's duties probably approximated those he previously executed as a plantation inspector with the Freedmen's Bureau. Smith seems to have remained as a warden through 1875 when he was listed as residing at the corner of Perilliat and Magnolia.[35] A New Orleans map of that era shows the City Work House as fronting on Perilliat from Liberty to Magnolia Street.

The Metropolitan Police had a dual role. Law enforcement and general public safety tasks were the norm but the force also acted as a Republican militia when required. Superintendent A. S. Badger could muster about 500 Metropolitan Police plus a large number of black militia to meet major disruptions caused by White Leaguers, Conservative Democrats and other dissidents. Since such mobilizations included all available Metropolitan Police it is certain that James L. Smith was involved.[36]

In September, 1874, the steamer *Mississippi* docked in New Orleans with a shipment of arms intended for the Conservative Democrats and the White League. Governor Kellog ordered the Metropolitan Police to prevent the distribution of these weapons. A riot followed wherein at least 500 police and 300 black militia were routed and driven from the city. Order was restored by the army several days later and the Metropolitan Police were reinstated although eleven members were killed. The event came to be called the "Battle of Liberty Place" and the scene was just a few blocks from the City Work House. Smith's involvement in the event is unknown but what a tumultuous time it must have been.

In 1874, just prior to Smith's assignment as a warden, he was involved in an incident that resulted in accusations of murder with the suggestion of perjury and departmental political intrigue. This situation may have been the reason for his assignment as a warden, perhaps as a reward for participation in political chicanery or as a form of administrative assignment because he could not be trusted with regular police duties.

A burglary gang was active in New Orleans and when they broke into the Phelps Grocery on May 19, 1874, their identity became known to detectives James L. Smith and Thomas Devereaux. Munson Alexander, an escaped convict, Benjamin Alexander, his brother, and James Bowman were accused of the crime. By May 21 the detectives had traced the two brothers to a house at Seventh and Carondelet Streets.[37]

That evening Detective Devereaux and a uniformed officer approached the rear of the hideout. Detective Smith entered the front door and heard shots in the back yard. He ran through the house and saw the Alexander brothers firing revolvers at Devereaux. Both Smith and Devereaux returned fire with their handguns. Munson Alexander was hit several times but managed to escape through a back alley. Benjamin Alexander was not hit by the gunfire and surrendered.[38]

Following this affray, Devereaux swore out a complaint against Munson Alexander charging him with assault with intent to commit murder. The court approved the complaint and issued an arrest warrant. Alexander was now wanted for that crime in addition to burglary and escape from prison. Although wounded he continued to remain at large and was sheltered by friends.

Detectives Smith and Devereaux, with the aid of informants, soon determined Alexander's probable hiding place. On the evening of May 23 they went to police headquarters and obtained two double-barreled shotguns from the armory. The weapons were carefully loaded with buckshot charges and were carried by the detectives to a house on Feret Street. That vacant building had been rented for them by the Superintendent of Police earlier in the day and it was an excellent neighborhood surveillance location.[39]

At three o'clock the next morning Munson Alexander left a building on Feret Street and came into view. The detectives rushed into the street and called for his surrender. Alexander drew a pistol as he turned to run. Detective Smith fired one shot over Alexander's head while Devereaux fired both of his barrels directly at the fleeing criminal. Alexander fell dead on the cobblestone street. The body was taken to the police station and Smith made a full report of the event.[40]

The Coroner ordered an immediate autopsy to be conducted by Doctor C. P. Ames. At the following inquest it was determined that ten of the thirteen buckshot pellets in Alexander's body were in his back. Three wounds from revolver bullets were found to be from the previous encounter with Smith and Devereaux. Doctor Ames died just after the inquest and most of his records on this case disappeared.[41]

The inquest held no one liable and after the body was released to relatives no further actions were taken in regard to the incident. Smith must have been given the assignment as warden shortly afterward as street directory listings were usually made in early or mid-summer.

Eighteen months later New Orleans was shocked to read that James L. Smith and Thomas Devereaux were accused of murdering Munson Alexander. Testimony, prior to a Grand Jury hearing, was taken in the Municipal Police Court on November 13, 1875. The evidence revealed that, while Smith's original oral and written reports claimed that Alexander was shot when he drew a pistol and fled after being ordered to halt, he now recanted that account. His new version held that Alexander had stopped and raised his hands in surrender, then Devereaux shot him in the back.[42]

Before the hearing ended some thirty witnesses were called. Accusations were made that Smith had bragged of shooting Alexander, that Devereaux was incriminating Smith to exonerate himself and that others were involved in covering up the facts. The primary issues that could not be resolved were: (1) whether the one shot fired by Smith was into the air or at Alexander, (2) whether Devereaux fired both barrels at a fleeing or surrendering criminal, and (3) the reason Smith recanted his previous report and alleged that Devereaux wrongfully shot Alexander. The court opined that as many as three or four other persons were implicated and should be tried. Perhaps the judge was implying that the administration of the Metropolitan Police were involved. The matter was sent on to the Grand Jury.

Smith was out on bail and a witness in another court shortly thereafter. The case involved a burglary prosecution against one Matt Hogan. Smith's testimony against Hogan was challenged by the defense and his reputation was attacked because of his apparent falsification in the Devereaux matter. Such a challenge presented a serious threat to his value as a detective on the Metropolitan Police.[43]

Later, when the Alexander murder case finally came before the Grand Jury, both Devereaux and Smith were given a "Not a True Bill" verdict and were cleared of all charges. Apparently there was an unsolvable problem connected with requiring the two defendants to testify against each other and they were the only witnesses actually present at Alexander's shooting.[44] Nothing from the Grand Jury deliberations was preserved that would explain the reasons behind Smith's accusations against Devereaux but there are several possibilities.

The Metropolitan Police were plagued by internal strife and political intrigue. Thomas Devereaux was personable, talented and politically active. Perhaps elements of the bureaucracy felt threatened and connived with Smith to accuse Devereaux of a crime that would eliminate him from the force without the appearance of a political vendetta. Smith's appointment as Warden of the City Work House may have been somehow connected with such a plot.

Another theory could hold that Smith was greatly troubled that he had initially misreported facts to protect his friend. While shielding his comrade, the man who was witness and best man at his wedding, seemed necessary at the time of the incident, following events may have changed Smith's mind. Perhaps Devereaux later revealed himself to be untrustworthy and corrupt. Smith may have felt guilty over the spurious report. If such were the case, perhaps Smith's recantation was an attempt to soothe his conscience and right an unpunished wrong.

Consider also the possibility that Smith actually did shoot Alexander instead of firing into the air as he reported. Smith may have changed his story to insure that the entire blame fell on Devereaux. Although recanting his report might endanger the balance of his career with the Metropolitan Police, it would be preferable to the penalty for murder. In any event, nothing more was found of Smith's activities in New Orleans after January, 10, 1876.

A combination of events probably combined to end Smith's employment with the Metropolitan Police. In February, 1876, Smith's one-time friend and former co-defendant Thomas Devereaux was indicted for the murder of former detective Robert Harris. This incident followed an attempt on Devereaux's life in a murder plot planned by Harris. Concurrently, with the withdrawal of military reconstruction forces and the Federal election of 1876, the Democrats reclaimed power and began to replace Metropolitan Police personnel with officers from their own party.[45]

Coincidently, the Louisiana State Legislature convened a committee in 1876 to examine corruption allegations against members of the Metropolitan Police. Testimony revealed that, in October, 1872, Special Officer Smith was given $25 and allowed to charge a new hat from a store in the Saint Charles Hotel. This bribe was to ignore a crime against a sailor in the Alhambra Saloon. The incident was but one of many cited against members and former members of the Metropolitan Police.[46]

The changes planned by the Democratic Party, Smith's testimony problems in the Alexander case, the corruption hearings and the implication of his former friend in another murder probably combined to cause detective James L. Smith to leave New Orleans for employment with the Union Pacific Railway at Omaha, Nebraska.

Thomas Devereaux was acquitted of murdering Detective Harris but was terminated from the newly reorganized police department. He then became a state legislator and eventually returned to New Orleans as Chief of Detectives. Devereaux later feuded with David and Mike Hennessey, detectives under his supervision, and was killed in an 1881 gunfight with them.[47] Smith's activities throughout the rest of his life reflect that he shared Devereaux's violent, combative and belligerent temperament.

4

NEBRASKA

OMAHA, NEBRASKA, BECAME closely linked to the Union Pacific Railway in 1863 when President Lincoln declared that city would be the eastern terminus of the proposed transcontinental railroad. Construction began in 1865 and was completed at Promontory Point, Utah, in 1869. That accomplishment placed the Union Pacific in a key position to capitalize on the nation's westward expansion and many of the related commercial business opportunities.

James L. Smith and his wife doubtlessly traveled north from New Orleans by steamboat to St. Louis and then up the Missouri River to Omaha. The 1876-77 Omaha street directory listed James as a Union Pacific Railway employee at the corner of Pacific and Fifth Streets. Anna Smith resided at 557 Eleventh Street, a short distance away and her occupation was shown as a washerwoman.[48] The location shown for Smith was next to the Union Pacific rail yards and was probably the railway's police headquarters. The street directory must have recorded him at his work location instead of with Anna on Eleventh Street. Perhaps Smith was assigned to depot or rail yard security as was later the case at Cheyenne, Wyoming.

Smith's ability to obtain employment so quickly with the Union Pacific implies some previous connection with the railroad industry or influential managers. The depression of 1873 drove eighty-nine of the nations 364 railroads into bankruptcy. By 1876 national unemployment had risen to fourteen percent and railroad strikes were a threat.[49] In the face of these conditions Smith was able to obtain a well paying position on short notice. Might his possible past employment with the Baltimore & Ohio Railroad have played a role?

Protection for Union Pacific interests was established through their detective force. These private officers were also commissioned as peace officers that could act off railroad property and had the legal authority to serve warrants and make arrests. Railroad detectives often worked sub-rosa to develop informants or penetrate outlaw gangs.[50]

The Union Pacific tried to avoid publicity about their detective force and discouraged mention of them in newspaper articles. Nevertheless, by 1877 it was publicly known that James L. Smith, N. K. Boswell, George Eisley and M. F. Leach were Union Pacific detectives. Whispering Smith, as he soon came to be known in the west, was often referred to as the deputy sheriff from Cheyenne because he held that commission.[51]

James L. Smith was assigned to duties at the Union Pacific depot in Cheyenne, Wyoming, by early 1878. The railroad wished to improve passenger security and was concerned with the vagrants, pickpockets and drunks that frequented the depot. As was the custom with Union Pacific detectives, Smith was commissioned as a special policeman by the City of Cheyenne.[52]

At some point during 1878 Smith investigated an embezzlement of Union Pacific funds by one of their employees and one J. G. Mills, a local newspaperman. Nothing came of the investigation but hard feelings developed between Mills and Smith. Mills, an employee of the local Cheyenne newspaper, was to extract his revenge later.

Although the details are not known, in February, 1879, Smith arrested one Robert Johnson and lodged him in the city jail. Johnson then accused Smith of stealing several dollars from him during the booking process. The Cheyenne newspaper, encouraged by Mills, featured a story that was very uncomplimentary to Smith. The evidence against Smith did not support the charge in court but the City Mayor launched his own investigation and determined that there was enough doubt of Smith's honesty that his commission should be revoked.[53]

This incident caused the Union Pacific some embarrassment and they had Smith deputized by the Laramie County Sheriff after which he was transferred to Sidney, Nebraska. Smith had by then developed a deep hatred for Mills and it was to smolder while other major events occupied his time.

The Union Pacific established the town of Sidney in 1867 as a rail yard and division point. Indian attacks required protection for railroad workers and Fort Sidney was built nearby. These soldiers and railroad workers attracted gambling dens, the liquor trade and prostitution to Sidney. The population exploded with the Black Hills gold rush and desperate characters were attracted by the possibilities. The town became wide open. At one point there were twenty-three saloons among the eighty-nine establishments selling liquor.

Once settled in at Sidney, Whispering Smith was assigned to help hunt down Doc Middleton, the leader of a horse-stealing gang that was the curse of stockmen throughout the Nebraska Panhandle. Ranchers, stage lines and Indian reservations were numbered among his victims. Middleton, a Texan, was in addition suspected of killing a soldier during a dispute in Sidney. Local ranchers determined to stop Middleton's rampage and offered generous rewards for his capture. The Union Pacific supported this effort by offering manpower to support the various posses. Whispering Smith was assigned to lead one posse in the Spring of 1879 and was accompanied by three other Union Pacific detectives. They swept the area north of Sidney to the Niobrara River and then rode east for ten days without encountering Middleton.[54]

Another posse working with Smith's group was headed by Sheriff Robert Hughes of Keith County, Nebraska. He found Middleton's trail and followed it toward Sidney. The posses located Middleton's gang at a camp about two miles west of town. Sheriff Hughes notified officers at Sidney and held the posses at a distance from the camp to await arrival of the Cheyenne County Sheriff from Sidney.[55]

Plans were laid to lure the Middleton gang into Sidney where they could be trapped. It was felt that a raid on their camp would only scatter the outlaws and many would escape. Charley Reed, a gambler known to the gang, was induced to visit the camp and tempt them with tales of the decadence to be found in town. He was successful only in enticing one outlaw, Joseph Smith, to visit Sidney. When the pair arrived, riding double on Reed's horse, posse members surrounded them and attempted to arrest Joseph Smith. He tried to flee and was fatally shot by a posse member. Although a coroner's jury did not name the shooter, a local historian holds that it was Whispering Smith.[56] Sheriff Hughes, discouraged by the inept affair in Sidney, moved against Middleton's camp but he was too late and the posses were again in pursuit of the outlaws.

William C. Lykens was stock inspector for the Wyoming Stock Growers Association. He was motivated by the various rewards offered for Middleton's capture and wanted to be included on the posses that were searching the Nebraska panhandle. He resigned his position as a stock inspector and became a Union Pacific detective. William H. Llewellyn, a federal agent assigned to stop rustling on Indian reservations, was also intent on capturing Middleton. To that end he and Lykens conspired with one Lyman Hazen, an ex-convict associate of Middleton, to organize a meeting to discuss the possibility of his surrender and later pardon.

The affair came to a head on Sunday, July 20, 1879, when a gunfight disrupted the planned meeting. There are almost as many versions of this event as there were participants. Hazen and Middleton were wounded. Llewellyn fled to Fort Hartstuff for help and Lykens rode into Columbus, Nebraska. Middleton, assisted by members of his outlaw gang, was helped to safety on one side of the Niobrara River. Hazen was sheltered on the other side by homesteaders. Both were treated by the same doctor that came from O'Neill City, over fifty miles away.

When Llewellyn reached Fort Hartstuff he organized a return force that was eventually composed of troopers and peace officers including union Pacific detectives Lykens, Leach and Whispering Smith.[57] On July 27 this posse located and arrested the wounded Middleton and took him to Sidney. After treatment he was arraigned in a local court and remanded to Cheyenne for trial because many of Middleton's crimes were committed in Wyoming and he had too many friends in Sidney. Fear that the outlaw element might try to rescue him prompted a public warning that anyone who interfered would be shot. Whispering Smith and Llewellyn bore Middleton to the train on a stretcher. They were preceded by Lykens who carried a double-barreled shotgun and two Colt forty-five caliber revolvers.[58]

Middleton was sentenced to five years in prison at the conclusion of his trial in Cheyenne. The sentence was ordered to be served at the Nebraska State Penitentiary because a fire had closed the Wyoming Territorial Prison. On September 30, 1879, Middleton was placed on a train for the Nebraska Penitentiary at Lincoln, Nebraska. His escort included heavily armed Laramie County Sheriff Draper and Whispering Smith.[59]

Outlawry had become pandemic along the border between Nebraska and the Wyoming and Dakota Territories during the 1870s. Livestock thefts threatened the solvency of ranching operations and frequent robberies along the stage lines to the Black Hills endangered the local economy. The Union Pacific Railway had a stake in protecting both these activities because a large portion of their freight business depended on the gold strike and cattle shipments. Law enforcement in the area was thinly spread and ineffective. Petitions from the affected areas pled for protection and one such warned that thefts of horse herds from the Pine Ridge Reservation might precipitate another Indian war. In addition, stagecoach robbery had become a deadly affair. The general public had become the personal victims of the outlaws and endangered stagecoach guards became enraged. Several vigilante or regulator groups were formed and a newspaper actually editorialized that stage robbers would be lynched if caught.[60]

By the Spring of 1879 the United States Department of Justice had appointed William H. Llewellyn as a special agent to investigate the theft of Indian livestock, liquor violations and miscellaneous other federal crimes. Llewellyn was previously an employee of the Omaha Police Department and had strong political recommendations for the federal appointment.

This newly appointed agent immediately began the previously mentioned investigation of the notorious horse thief, Doc Middleton. Early in the pursuit and arrest of Middleton, Llewellyn was assisted by a variety of officers, one of whom was Whispering Smith, the Union Pacific detective still commissioned as a deputy sheriff by Laramie County Wyoming.

Coincidentally, when consulting about crime problems with Dr Valentine McGillycuddy, the agent in charge of the Pine Ridge Reservation, Llewellyn suggested that Whispering Smith be requested on loan from the Union Pacific.[61] Smith's reputation for taking direct action and achieving results had apparently impressed the new federal agent. This request was approved and Smith began to serve the interests of the reservation as time permitted during the Middleton affair.

The reservation at Lone Pine was originally established to shelter the Sioux that earlier moved from Minnesota to the Black Hills area. These Indians traded their woodlands environment for the more open spaces and acquired horses to aid in their hunt for buffalo. Horse herds became the measure of Sioux wealth and status. The theft of herds by outlaws presented a threat to the peace because if the thefts were not stopped by authorities the Indians might do it themselves. It was feared that the mistakes and revenge inherent in tribal action would precipitate another Indian war.

Stagecoach routes connecting the Black Hills to Cheyenne, Sidney and the Union Pacific railroad skirted the Pine Ridge Reservation. During 1878 and 1879 several stagecoaches were held up by a gang whose leader had a noticeable limp. He was called "Lame Johnny" but he was actually Cornelius Donahue, alias John Hurley, a college man from the east. Lame Johnny had been a horse thief in Texas before his arrival at Deadwood City and was wanted for murder there. The horse herds on the Red Cloud Reservation near Pine Ridge soon tempted Lame Johnny and he raided them several times killing a guard on one occasion. This type of incident was exactly what McGillycuddy wanted Llewellyn and Smith to stop.

Lame Johnny was also tempted by the Deadwood

stages that transported thousands of dollars and loads of gold bars in armored coaches. A clique or fraternity of guards known as the "Shotgun Brigade" protected these routes. It consisted of Boone and Jim May, Gale Hill, Ross Davis and Jesse Brown among others.[62] These men were all well known to Whispering Smith as he had worked with them previously. They were to be brought together again in July, 1879, by the activities of Lame Johnny.

Reservation Agent McGillycuddy learned through tribal sources that Lame Johnny was planning another raid on Indian horse herds and that he was presently in the vicinity of Fort Sheridan. McGillycuddy quickly wired Captain Emmet Crawford, the Commander of that installation, and requested him to find and arrest Lame Johnny and his outlaw friends.

Crawford located and arrested two men that he believed to be the ones that McGillycuddy sought. He wired the agent to send someone to identify these suspected outlaws and transport them to civil custody. A wire was sent by McGillycuddy to Sidney where Whispering Smith was on Union Pacific business. Smith was requested to proceed to Fort Sheridan, determine if the two prisoners were actually the Lame Johnny and Frank Harris that were wanted for robbery and horse theft.[63] This assignment is another indication of the respect held for Smith's knowledge of local outlaws.

The judge of the Dakota Territory District Court had appointed McGillycuddy as a court commissioner.

This title carried with it the authority to issue warrants, hold preliminary hearings and remand prisoners for trial at Deadwood City. This authority came into use three days later when Whispering Smith arrived at Pine Ridge to assure the agent that the arrested men were Lame Johnny and Frank Harris. McGillycuddy told Smith that these two men had been a constant threat to the reservation and that he'd be glad to get rid of them. Smith was issued a warrant of commitment and instructed to transport the outlaws to Deadwood City for trial. At that time Smith was said to have told McGillycuddy that he might just lose the prisoners along the way. Smith was then alleged to have sent a wire to the Shotgun Brigade asking them to intercept the stage that would transport Lame Johnny at Buffalo Gap.[64]

The two prisoners had been transferred to Fort Robinson and Smith arranged for a special stage to meet him there for the transportation assignment. It was decided that it would be too dangerous to take both outlaws at the same time through an area where Lame Johnny's gang was still active. Smith chose to take Lame Johnny first, and return later for Harris but the safety of the prisoner may not really have been his concern.

Jesse Brown, a very experienced shotgun guard, was asked to ride as a horseback escort. Brown's wife and two children were approved by Smith as additional passengers, presumably for a free trip to Deadwood City. As the stage left Fort Robinson on the evening of July 1, 1879, it contained Smith, Lame Johnny, Mrs. Brown and the children plus an armed driver. Jesse Brown rode ahead to protect the stage.[65]

All went well until about eleven o'clock when the stage was eight miles north of Buffalo Gap. Suddenly a mixed group of vigilantes jumped from the brush alongside the road and ordered the driver to stop. The driver obeyed and the vigilantes demanded the surrender of Lame Johnny. Whispering Smith leaped from the stage to protest but was overcome and forced to drop his revolver. Lame Johnny was taken away from the stage while Smith, the driver and the other passengers were ordered to remain beside it. Lame Johnny was taken about one hundred yards away to a large tree. Smith followed and demanded that the group at least allow him to recover his handcuffs before they hung his prisoner. They generously agreed and Smith then returned to the stage ostensibly to search for his revolver. This took quite some time and after he found it he returned to the tree and found Lame Johnny hanging by the neck. The vigilantes were long gone.[66] The suspicion that the vigilantes were actually members of the Shotgun Brigade permeates the event.

Jesse Brown, the horseback guard that was supposed to provide a protective escort, arrived at the coach just as Smith returned from viewing Lame Johnny's body at the hanging tree. Brown claimed that he was warned off the trail by a voice from the side of the road and, when he felt it safe to do so, started back toward the coach to help Smith. He was delayed because he encountered his family fleeing back along the road and felt it more important to help them.[67]

The survivors of the incident all boarded the stage and it proceeded to Rapid City where Smith reported the lynching and began to organize a second trip to transport Frank Harris. The next day Lame Johnny's body was found swinging from a tree limb by passing drovers and they buried him next to a stream bed that is now called Lame Johnny Creek.[68]

When Frank Harris learned of Lame Johnny's fate he attempted to escape from the guardhouse at Fort Robinson. He was quickly recaptured, thanks to the vigilance of the sergeant in charge, and was available when Whispering Smith returned for him. The second prisoner transportation was made without incident.[69]

The implication that the lynching of Lame Johnny was a planned event is inescapable. Smith's telegram to the Shotgun Brigade, his prediction about losing a prisoner, McGillycuddy's expressed desire to be rid of the troublesome rustlers and newspaper support for hanging such outlaws all suggest a plot. One element remains unclear. Why did Jesse Brown endanger his family by taking them along on such a potentially dangerous trip? Perhaps he wanted to establish a defense should he be accused of complicity in the lynching. He could claim the he would not have included his family on a trip where he had the slightest expectation of danger.

The suspicion that Jesse Brown had a tendency to

conspire with others to lynch stage robbers and outlaws relates to an October, 31, 1878, incident that may also have involved Whispering Smith. Billy Mansfield and Archie McLaughlin were identified as stagecoach robbers and were in custody at Fort Laramie, Wyoming. They were alleged to be members of the "Big Nose George Gang" and were to be transported through Cheyenne for trial at Deadwood City. George Parrott, known as "Big Nose George" because of his large and distinctive nose, headed a gang that attempted a train robbery near Carbon, Wyoming. Two members of the posse that responded were killed and Parrott's gang was hunted down with a vengeance. One member, Dutch Charley Burris, was arrested and later lynched at Carbon. A similar fate awaited Parrott at Rawlings, Wyoming.

Mansfield and McLaughlin were put in the custody of Jim May and Jesse Brown, members of the Shotgun Brigade, and they left Fort Laramie by stage. According to Brown and May, they were stopped within a mile of the fort by masked vigilantes who disarmed them and hung their prisoners.[70]

A different description of the event is offered by Kennett Harris in his memoirs. He claims that Whispering Smith was assigned to transport the two outlaws and chose to do it alone. Smith is supposed to have turned into a cottonwood grove, hung both prisoners, then claimed that he had been stopped by masked vigilantes who took the prisoners from him[71] Harris wrote this article thirty-seven years after the incident and it is not certain if he relied on memory or if he consulted journal notes written at the time. In any event, his reminiscence indicates how the local populace regarded Smith and his reputation in the area. The possibility that Smith was involved is enhanced somewhat because he was assigned to Cheyenne by the Union Pacific at the time of the incident and that railroad had a vested interest in the security of stage lines to the gold fields.

Elimination of criminals by extra-judicial means was also occasionally done by Whispering Smith's associates. Later, in February, 1880, Llewellyn and Boone May arrested Lou "Curley" Grimes who was previously involved with Lame Johnny and Doc Middleton. Grimes was transported to court by Llewellyn and May in a stage coach. His guards claimed that Grimes asked for his handcuffs to be removed because the bitter cold was freezing his hands. This was done and as the stage entered the Fort Meade Reservation he sprang out and fled into the foliage alongside the road. His body was riddled by gunfire and he fell dead in the snow. The shooting took place on a military reservation and seemed suspicious. Llewellyn and May were indicted and tried for murder but were acquitted as there were no other witnesses to contradict their story.[72]

With the end of Lame Johnny and with Doc Middleton's fate sealed, the Union Pacific once again assigned Whispering Smith to Cheyenne. In October, 1879, he began a public denunciation campaign against his old adversary, J. G. Mills. Smith had learned, possibly through correspondence with former associates in the Freedmen's Bureau, that Mills was from Lexington, Mississippi. He further learned that Mills was a member of the White League and had been involved in the murder of a former slave.

On November 11, 1879, the two antagonists met on the streets of Cheyenne and Mills denied Smith's accusations. In a heated quarrel, fueled by liquor, Smith challenged Mills to arm himself for a duel at a park near the lake. Mills denied that he was a duelist. Smith warned him to be armed when next seen and Mills walked away.

Smith went to the lake prepared to duel but when Mills did not appear he returned to town loudly denouncing Mills as a coward. Mills, however, had taken Smith's warning and armed himself with a Sharps rifle. Whispering Smith saw Mills approach with the Sharps under his arm and decided the odds were against him since he had only a revolver. Smith jumped a fence and hid in a nearby yard. A city policeman arrived and took both men before a judge. At least this is the version reported in the newspaper that employed Mills.[73]

The Nebraska town of Sidney became very important with the 1876 gold discovery in the Black Hills of the Dakota Territory. Sidney's location on the Union Pacific Railway made for the closest stage and wagon connection to the gold fields. By 1877 about 1,500 people a day passed through Sidney on their way to or from Deadwood City and points north.

A large gold shipment arrived at Sidney on the evening of March 9, 1880 in an armored stage coach named "Old Ironsides." This coach was fortified with half-inch boilerplate, had gun ports and was used only for transportation of gold and currency. It was guarded by Scott Davis, his brother Ross, Boone May, Jesse Brown and Gail Hill, all members of the Shotgun Brigade. The plan was to load the gold cargo into the express car of a Union Pacific train that was scheduled to depart that afternoon. The heavy load and muddy roads combined to slow their trip and they were too late for the train connection.[74]

The station agent, Chester K. Allen, told Davis that the shipment would have to be held overnight to be loaded on the first morning train. Allen unlocked the express office vault room and the heavy cargo was stacked inside. Davis expressed some doubt about the security involved and, although Allen had given him a receipt for the gold, Davis assigned Boone May and Gale Hill to guard the building overnight.[75]

Early the next morning the gold was removed from the vault and placed on a baggage cart in the freight room to await the arrival of the train. When the train did not arrive by noon it was decided that everyone should go to a nearby hotel for lunch. Allen vouched for the security of the freight room and locked the door.

Allen found the gold gone when he returned to the station shortly after noon. Davis and his men searched the building and found that a hole had been cut in the freight room floor from the crawl space below. Tracks in the fresh snow led to a coal pile under which some of the gold bricks were found. All the shipment was recovered except for two gold bricks and some currency, a loss of about $13,000.[76]

Davis and his men immediately began an investigation although his crew was not responsible for the loss because the station agent had signed a receipt for the gold. Later that day General Superintendent Morsman of the Pacific Express Company and John Thurston arrived by train from Cheyenne. Thurston was an attorney for the Union pacific and would come to be closely involved with Whispering Smith in the months to follow. The next train brought Robert Law, Superintendent of Union Pacific's Mountain Division and the Union Pacific detective, James L. Smith.[77]

Whispering Smith's preliminary investigation indicated that four men were involved in the theft; former Cheyenne County Sheriff Cornelius McCarty, Patsy Walters, Dennis Flannagan and Chester Allen. McCarty came to Sidney in the mid-1870s and was elected County Coroner by 1874. He then served as County Sheriff in 1876 and 1877. Graft and income from his Capital Saloon and Gambling Hall, as well as profits from a cattle herd funded a mansion he built at nearby Lodgepole and gave him great local influence. The Capitol Saloon and Gambling Hall was the largest such establishment in Sidney. This structure later became the Tobin Building and is now on the National Register of Historic Places.

McCarty had gathered about him a gang, most of

whom were suspected of the gold theft. Patrick Walters was a bartender at the Capitol Saloon and managed that business. Dennis Flannagan was a local barber that McCarty used as a front man for various financial manipulations. Also a part of the gang was Thomas Ryan, formerly a deputy sheriff under McCarty. Ryan was the County Assessor the year of the gold theft and absconded with a good share of the county treasury.[78]

Whispering Smith was only able to develop circumstantial evidence against his suspects but did succeed in having John M. Thurston, the legal representative for the Union Pacific, appointed as special prosecutor. Among the obstacles to prosecution were: (1) the grand jury tampering done by a member, Dennis Flannagan, (2) obstructions by the county judge who also worked as a faro dealer at the Capitol Saloon and Gambling Hall, and (3) a goodly portion of the local population that was indifferent to crime and corruption. The evidence against Chester Allen was strongest and he was held for trial. Indictments for all the others failed.

Whispering Smith was furious at the outcome of his efforts. He was convinced of the gang's guilt and very antagonistic toward those who obstructed the prosecution. On the evening of May 24, 1880, Smith entered Doran and Tobin's Saloon for an evening of card playing and drinking with several acquaintances. After several hours the group began to harmonize old songs. Patrick Walters, the bar tender at the Capitol Saloon, was present and began to mock the singers. A quarrel ensued during which Walters called one of the singers, probably Smith, a thief. Smith, angry with Walters over the gold robbery case, could no longer contain his rage and drew a Webley forty-five caliber revolver from his coat pocket and demanded to know who Walters was calling a thief. Walters responded that Smith was the thief he meant and drew his revolver. Smith shot him once in the abdomen and missed with a second shot. Walters got his first shot off just as Smith fired a third time. Walters' bullet struck and disabled Smith's Webley, then glanced up into his wrist and arm. Walters fired three more wild shots as he fell to the floor. He was later treated by a doctor who considered the wound in his abdomen to be fatal and predicted a lingering death.[79]

Whispering Smith was afraid of quick retaliation by McCarty's gang and fled to the hotel room of his friends, Scott and Ross Davis. Sidney law officers attempted to arrest Smith there but the stage coach guards interceded and promised to deliver him to jail the next morning after medical treatment. When Smith surrendered himself the next day he carried a rifle and was permitted to keep it in the cell for self-protection, a vivid commentary on law and order in old Sidney.

In court, Smith's account of the affair held that he was leaving the saloon when Walters called him a thief and drew a revolver. Smith claimed they fired simultaneously and denied he had antagonized or spoken to Walters previously. Bail was set at $10,000 and promptly posted by his supporters. The Union Pacific attorney intervened and the charges were dropped on the grounds of self-defense. Smith's injury healed during the summer months and he had no further violent encounters with the McCarty gang although there was a continuing undercurrent of hostility. Walters recovered from his wound and remained in the Sidney area but avoided any contact with Smith. It has not been determined where Smith's wife resided during his assignments in the Cheyenne and Sidney areas.

The trial of Chester Allen was completed on October 29, 1880, and a friendly jury found him not guilty. His connection with the McCarty gang was never revealed. During the trial Whispering Smith met every night with the prosecutor, John Thurston, to discuss the day's testimony. These meetings were held under unusual circumstances that reveal a bit about Smith's personality. Instead of meeting in Thurston's private car furnished by the Union Pacific, Smith insisted that they walk along the tracks to a lonely section where in a whisper he would confer with the attorney. Here we have a clue as to the voice pattern that earned Smith his nick-name and his obsession with secrecy. During these meetings Smith pled for permission to kill McCarty.[80]

By the end of the year Smith's feud with the McCarty gang began to intensify. He wrote an anonymous letter that was published in the Sidney *Plaindealer* that accused Flannagan of being a troublemaking associate of McCarty who blocked grand jury indictments in the gold robbery case. Flannagan was enraged and set out to learn who was responsible for the libelous letter.

On December 31, 1880, Flannagan began a drinking spree that extended into New Year's morning. He somehow learned that Smith was responsible for publication of the letter and by four o'clock on New Year's Day he marched toward the Lockwood House intent on a confrontation. As he entered the lobby he made threats against Smith and exhibited a revolver. Smith was just finishing a meal in the dinning room and as he entered the lobby Flannagan approached him to demand that they meet privately in a small room next to the bar.

Multiple shots were heard just after the pair entered the room. Flannagan burst back out the door crying that he'd been shot and then fell to the floor. He was taken to another nearby hotel and treated for three mortal gunshot wounds. Whispering Smith was arrested and claimed self-defense. As in the Walters incident he was quickly freed through the efforts of the Union Pacific.[81]

That railway had grown tired of the crime and violence in Sidney but they were also sensitive to the negative publicity Whispering Smith was creating. The General Manager of the Union Pacific, S. H. Clark, immediately recalled Smith to Cheyenne and advised the town of Sidney that if they failed to eliminate the crime and corruption the rail line would be relocated through another town. The ultimatum prodded local citizens, most of whom depended on railroad commerce, to form a vigilante group called

The Regulators. In April a notice was signed by sixty-four of them that warned the criminal element to leave town.

SAFETY IS THE WATCHWORD

Lawlessness in Sidney has run riot long enough. The lives and property of law-abiding people have been endangered to an extent that it has become insufferable. Officers have been powerless and the law defied, robberies have been committed in our midst with impunity; arson has been attempted in the heart of town, attempted assassination has been winked at, the lives of our best citizens threatened, and every rule of order and decency trampled under foot. Thus the peaceable and law abiding people have been driven to the necessity of organizing for self protection and the rescue of our town from the grasp and dictum of lawlessness...Thousands of dollars paid into our treasury have been wasted in a farcical effort to punish criminals. It has been so glaring an outrage and so burdensome to the county, that the town is threatened by the railroad company that if it is not stopped they will remove their buildings and allow the town to die of dry rot...ALL MURDERERS, THIEVES, PIMPS, AND SLEEK FINGERED "GENTLEMEN" MUST GO.[82]

The Regulators and local officers raided the Capitol Saloon following this notice and jailed McCarty plus a number of his followers. A few nights later a mob stormed the jail and removed the prisoners. They took John MacDonald to a telegraph pole and hung him. He had aroused the ire of an already angry community by shooting at Deputy Sheriff McIntosh during the raid on the Capitol Saloon. The rest of the prisoners, including McCarty and Walters, were horsewhipped and run out of town under the threat of hanging if they returned. Whispering Smith returned to Sidney the night of MacDonald's lynching. When nothing was heard of the exiled McCarty thereafter it was thought that Smith followed him out of town for a killing. This rumor was strengthened because Smith disappeared for two days following the lynching.[83]

One theory about Smith's presence in Sidney on the night of the lynching had to do with MacDonald's robbery of a Black Hills stage coach. Some felt that Smith engineered the lynching because MacDonald evaded conviction on a case investigated by the railroad detective. This connection relates to the conviction of Fritz Staurck and John MacDonald for the June 9, 1878, robbery of a stage coach near Buffalo Gap. Frank Harris, Lame Johnny's old crime partner, was convicted one day after

Staurch and MacDonald. He immediately confessed to the crime for which those two were convicted and both outlaws were released by order of the court.[84] MacDonald drifted to Sidney, probably attracted to its general state of lawlessness, and fit into the saloon trade. If Whispering Smith precipitated MacDonald's lynching the motive may have been to administer delayed justice.

Whispering Smith began to drink heavily following MacDonald's lynching. From his attitude and remarks it was suspected that he had been involved in the deed. In a heated argument with two prominent Sidney citizens over the hanging he became angry and drew a revolver accusing them of being no better than MacDonald and also deserving to be hung.[85]

Smith was quickly disarmed and taken before a county judge who fined him fifty dollars for creating a disturbance and drunkenness. A delegation of citizens then met Smith as he was leaving the courthouse and gave him ten minutes to leave town under penalty of hanging. Smith quickly boarded a westbound train for Cheyenne. The local newspaper stated that should he return to Sidney he would be lynched by citizens who considered him a fatal mischief-maker.[86] This editorial comment indicates the degree to which it was felt that Whispering Smith had conducted his own violent vendetta against the criminal element in Sidney.

It is probable that this incident, combined with the Flannagan and Walters shootings, caused Smith to leave his employment with the Union Pacific to seek other opportunities in the west. Regrettably, no personnel or operational records exist for this early period of Union Pacific history that can provide information on Smith's termination.[87]

Cornelius McCarty was never seen in Sidney again. He apparently abandoned his mansion at Lodgepole and arranged to have his family join him in exile. He was rumored to have fled to Idaho with his associate, Tom Ryan, and to have been killed there several years later. This may well be the case as his wife, Kate, was living alone in Boise, Idaho, in 1900. She is listed as a housekeeper with four McCarty children and miscellaneous borders. The two youngest children were born in Montana, 1889, and in Idaho, 1892.[88] Thus Cornelius McCarty must have been alive until at least 1891. His cohort, Thomas Ryan, is also listed in Boise as a prospector at age 53.[89]

The mystery of the unrecovered gold and currency taken in the Sidney robbery was later solved by Scott Davis, the stage coach guard. Several years after the robbery he chanced to met Bill Feen, a former member of McCarty's gang, during a trip to Chicago. Feen related that McCarty planned the robbery and, when most of the loot was found at the depot, he gave the remaining gold bricks to Feen for sale at Denver. Feen, and another former gang member named Dempsey, cut the bricks into pieces and sold them for $10,000. They gave none of the proceeds to McCarty who only gained about $1,000 in cash from the crime.[90]

Patrick Walters was shot twice in just three years. He fled from Sidney to Montana and worked at various jobs along the Northern Pacific Railroad between Bozeman and Fargo. It will be recalled that he was first shot by Whispering Smith on May 24, 1879, at Sidney. In that encounter one of Walters' bullets hit Smith's revolver and rendered it inoperable. One of Smith's shots hit Walters in the abdomen and while it appeared to be a mortal wound, he survived.

In the second incident Walters' revolver was disabled by the first shot fired by Hugo Hoppy in a February 22, 1883, Bozeman altercation. Hoppy's second shot hit Walters in the abdomen in almost exactly the same place as Smith's bullet had struck three years previously. Walters died the next day.[91]

Consider the coincidence. Walters was in two deadly encounters and in each case a revolver was disabled by an opponents shot. In both incidents Walters was shot in almost exactly the same place.

Doc Middleton was eventually released from prison and by June, 1884, he married and began to manage a saloon at Valentine, Nebraska. He became involved in the famous 1893 Chadron to Chicago Cowboy Horse Race promoted by John Maher and was thrust into the spotlight because of his criminal past. Although there were over twenty entrants only five riders actually started the grueling race. Middleton's horse failed him in Iowa and, while he did not win any prize money, he gained nationwide publicity. The balance of his life was spent in the saloon trade and he died in jail on December 27, 1913.[92]

Some have confused an event in 1878 involving Captain Eugene Smith with the activities of Whispering Smith. Both men were involved in similar roles in the same area. Gene Smith was a stage coach guard on the Black Hills to Cheyenne route during the time that the Union Pacific had Whispering Smith investigating crimes that affected travel to the gold fields.

On August 1, 1878, an elderly passenger on the Deadwood stage told a reporter from the *Sidney Telegraph* about an attempted robbery. A group of mounted bandits failed to stop a stage in which he was riding and they pursued it. The mounted guard, Captain Smith, engaged them in a running gunfight. The passenger estimated that the outlaws fired over fifty shots at Smith while he shot seventeen times with his rifle and four times with his revolver. "Out of respect for the Captain, I never saw such cool desperate courage exhibited in all my life," remarked the passenger.[93] Reports of this event caused some to believe Whispering Smith was the guard described but the article specifies that it was Eugene Smith.

The Stage Coach Museum at Lusk, Wyoming, lists Captain Gene Smith as one of a group of stage coach messengers known as the Shotgun Brigade along with Captain Scott Davis, Jesse Brown, Gale Hill and Billy Sample.[94] Note that the title of Captain is one that was often given to senior persons responsible for security and law enforcement during that era. It is probable that the two men knew each other because Whispering Smith had many relations with the Shotgun Brigade.

5

NEW MEXICO

THE TERRITORY OF NEW MEXICO was racked by turmoil in the late 1870s. A violent feud erupted between competing cattlemen and was exacerbated by commercial interests. Alexander McSween and John Tunstall challenged the Murphy-Dolan combine for control of water and grazing rights in the Lincoln County area. Open warfare resulted after Tunstall was murdered and dozens were killed. Western characters Pat Garrett and Billy the Kid became famous for their roles in this range war.

The death of Billy the Kid in 1881 and a grant of amnesty to all involved gradually brought an end to the feud but peace did not return to Lincoln County. Roving bands of renegade Mescalero

Apache Indians began to raid ranches for livestock and then return to the safety of their reservation. The ranchers demanded that the Bureau of Indian Affairs either control the outlaw Apaches or turn the problem over to the U. S. Army.

The Mescalero Reservation occupied over 450,000 acres near Tularosoa. It was authorized by President Ulysses S. Grant in 1873 but developed slowly because of difficulties between various Indian groups and inept management. It was decided not to use the army to control the renegade Apaches and instead, in June, 1881, William H. Llewellyn was appointed as an Indian Agent and charged with bringing order to the reservation. Llewellyn was immediately confronted with multiple crises. Squatters were illegally camped on reservation land and had begun to prospect for gold, the renegade Apache Nana was raiding nearby, a feud raged between sub-tribes and on the night he arrived there was a witch-burning.[95]

Llewellyn, quite familiar with the attributes of Whispering Smith from their joint involvement in the Doc Middleton and Lame Johnny affairs, requested that Smith be appointed as police chief for the reservation. He was hired as of June 23, 1881, in the rank of Chief Herder and Police Chief at a salary of $75 per month.[96] This employment opportunity seems to have been well timed with Smith's separation from the Union Pacific that followed the lynching of John MacDonald. It is unknown if Smith's wife accompanied him to New Mexico but the harsh conditions there make it unlikely.

Llewellyn and Whispering Smith quickly began to organize a police force for the reservation. Recommendations of tribal sub-chiefs, prominence on the reservation and prior experience were considerations in selection. A roster and pay scale was established on August 15, 1881, and included fifteen Mescalero Apache tribal members.

NAME	RANK	MONTHLY RATE
Peso	Captain	$8
Ramon Chi-quita	1st Lieutenant	$8
Charley	1st Sergeant	$5
Jose Tores	2nd Sergeant	$5
Big Rope	3rd Sergeant	$5
Bot-tel-la	Private	$5
Antonio	Private	$5
Domingo	Private	$5
Nicholas	Private	$5
Felix	Private	$5
Running Water	Private	$5
Patricio	Private	$5
Nu-ta-go-lin-je	Private	$5
Catarino	Private	$5
Ek-lo-de-na-in-ton	Private	$5[97]

No doubt the fear of raiding renegade Apaches speeded efforts to make the new police force operational. The most current threat was Nana, a Chiricahua Apache and compatriot of Victorio. Nana managed to escape with a group of followers when Victorio's band was destroyed by the Mexican Army. On July 13, 1881, he crossed into the United States near El Paso, Texas, and swept north on what historians would later call "Nana's Raid." His circular route drove up through New Mexico and covered over one thousand miles before re-entering Mexico. Nana's rampage was responsible for the death of approximately fifty settlers and as he passed near the Mescalero Reservation he was able to recruit twenty-five Mescalero Apaches.[98] Apparently the new reservation police force was unable to prevent this defection but managed to avoid a bloody confrontation and loss of life.

Supplies for the reservation were brought by wagon from the Atchison, Topeka and Santa Fe railhead at Las Cruces one-hundred miles to the south. One of Llewellyn's prime objectives for his new police force was to provide protection for these supplies. Whispering Smith organized and led an armed escort for the trip made on August 22, 1881, and established the procedures to be followed on subsequent trips. These wagon trains, escorted by armed Mescalero Indian Police, went unchallenged by outlaws and renegade Apaches from that time forward.[99]

Throughout the next year those Mescalero Apaches that left the reservation to take up the outlaw's life were a serious problem for Llewellyn and Smith. Give-Me-A-Horse, a Mescalero Apache prisoner at Fort Stanton, escaped and fled to the camp of a sub-chief, Nantizli. Another Apache outlaw, Carpio, murdered a sheepherder and also sought sanctuary in Nantizli's camp.[100]

Agent Llewellyn sent several messages to Nantzili that ordered him to surrender any fugitive Apaches that were sheltered in his camp. When Nantzili refused it was feared that this contempt for authority would weaken Llewellyn's ability to manage the reservation and encourage further misconduct. When negotiations failed a combined force consisting of reservation police and troopers from the 4th Cavalry stationed at Fort Stanton was formed. This improvised posse swept down on Nantzili's camp in an early morning raid. Resistance was encountered and gunfire flashed through the light of breaking dawn. Several wanted Apaches were captured but in the fight it was reported that Give-Me-A-Horse and Carpio were wounded by Whispering Smith and later died.[101]

A few wanted Apaches managed to escape the raid and were pursued by the posse. A second gunfight resulted in their capture but Llewellyn was wounded in the arm. The success of the raid brought some tranquility to the reservation and permitted Llewellyn to pursue his efforts in moving the Mescaleros to an agricultural economy while Whispering Smith devoted his time to routine reservation law enforcement.

Kennett Harris wrote his memories of Whispering

Smith in a 1915 article. In one of the incidents he describes the pursuit of a Mexican horse thief by Smith on the edge of the Mescalero Reservation. Smith captured him near Alamogordo, put a rope around his neck and led the horses toward a grove of trees. A Texas deputy sheriff that had also been following the thief arrived and demanded custody of the Mexican so that he could be returned to Texas for trial. Smith felt that was silly and argued for the more immediate course of action. The deputy won the argument and the Mexican was spared but the deputy expressed a fear of ever meeting Smith again. Harris claimed that Llewellyn felt that Smith was blood thirsty but accepted this trait because Smith got results.[102] Llewellyn, it will be recalled, had himself been previously accused of summary justice in the shooting of a prisoner.

At some point in 1882 Thomas Branigan replaced Peso as Captain of the Mescalero Reservation Police. He was a former prison guard in Ohio and the salary for the Indian Police must have been improved considerably for him to consider the position. When Smith left the Mescalero Reservation in 1883 or 1884 Branigan was promoted to the Chief's position.[103] There are a number of possible reasons for Smith's departure from the reservation but none so dramatic as those that caused his separation from the Metropolitan Police and the Union Pacific.

Edgar Beecher Bronson, a cattleman turned author, claims to have had a conversation with Whispering Smith when the unemployed detective visited him in El Paso,

Texas, shortly after leaving New Mexico. Bronson was the President of the West Texas Cattle Growers Association. Smith related that he was recruited to the Mescalero Reservation with promises of the type of action he liked. Peace, however, came too soon and there was little for him to do. When Llewellyn countermanded an order given by Smith to the Indian Police an altercation occurred between them and Smith resigned. Smith related that he drew his revolver on Llewellyn during that confrontation and the Indian Agent was lucky not to have accepted the challenge.[104]

In a different version of the event it is possible that the two fell out over the rewards for the Doc Middleton capture. Both Smith and Llewellyn received $200 at the close of that incident but later Llewellyn bragged that he'd actually been paid $10,000 by the Union Pacific.[105] While this claim lacks logic perhaps Smith learned of the boast and jealousy caused the quarrel. It was during this same El Paso meeting that Bronson claims Smith offered his services to the West Texas Cattle Growers Association. He proposed to solve their rustler problems cheap with no lawyer fees or court costs. Shortly after his El Paso visit Whispering Smith found employment with the Wyoming Cattle Growers Association. Perhaps he was referred to them by Bronson who was previously active with that group. It should be noted that Bronson's reminiscences sometimes fail the test of historical scrutiny. He was peripherally connected with the events he describes and while the situations may be accurate his roles in the occurrences may not completely be relied upon.[106]

Still another condition developed early in 1883 that may have contributed to Whispering Smith's departure from the Mescalero Reservation. Henry M. Teller, Secretary of the Interior, ordered that the Mescalero Reservation Police should be disarmed except for some old revolvers for which there was no modern ammunition. The Secretary may have come under the influence of eastern pro-Indian, anti-reservation activists. This order would render the police unable to execute their duties, according to correspondence by Agent Llewellyn.[107] Such a development would have been an affront to Smith's method of operation and a repudiation of his previous gunshot encounters with Indian outlaws.

Whispering Smith was rumored to have launched a torrid complaint through other channels and Llewellyn's letter was responded to by another change of policy. On June 22, 1883, the Commissioner of Indian Affairs ordered modern revolvers for the Mescalero Police. They were allotted thirty-six sets, each consisting of one forty-four caliber Remington Model 1875 revolver, holster, belt and fifty rounds of ammunition.[108] One might wonder how the government expected such a meager ammunition issue to support training and practice plus the requirements of service use.

Leon Metz claims Whispering Smith did not quit the Mescalero Reservation until 1884.[109] Whether he left in

1883 or 1884, his contemporaries soon followed. Thomas Branigan resigned as Chief of the Mescalero Indian Police and in 1885 he became a detective with the Texas Pacific Railroad. William H. Llewellyn continued as the Mescalero Indian Reservation Agent until 1885 when he resigned to practice law at Las Cruces, New Mexico. At the outset of the Spanish American War he joined Roosevelt's Rough Riders and served in Cuba as Captain of Troop H, 1st U. S. Volunteer Cavalry. After the war he became a close friend of President Theodore Roosevelt who appointed him as U. S. Attorney for New Mexico. Llewellyn was active in New Mexico politics until his death in 1927.[110]

It was thought by some that Whispering Smith returned to New Mexico in the early 1890s. His disagreements with Llewellyn over matters at the Mescalero reservation were thought to have been healed by the passage of time. Llewellyn had become a successful attorney in Las Cruces. In that same community a James Smith married the daughter of Silas Chatfield and became a rancher in the Sacramento Mountains near the Mescalero Reservation. This James Smith became involved in a property dispute with another rancher, Charles F. Hilton. On February 18, 1894, Hilton began to haul away some rails lying on Smith's ranch. A party, including Smith, his father-in-law and several others arrived and challenged the removal. Smith told Hilton that he was to be killed. Then Smith drew a revolver and shot Hilton three times.[111]

The confrontational manner of the murder, the

similarity of Smith's name, and the coincidental location of the incident caused some to believe Whispering Smith was the culprit. The shooting was certainly in his style but the assumption was incorrect. Genealogical research reveals that the shooter was actually James B. Smith, born in 1861 at Franklin, Missouri. When brought to trial he was defended by Albert B. Fall, an attorney later to be identified with the Teapot Dome scandal. James B. Smith won acquittal just as Whispering Smith did in all of his shooting scrapes.

6

WYOMING

WHISPERING SMITH'S EMPLOYment by the Wyoming Stock Growers Association quickly followed his departure from New Mexico. By 1884 he was again headquartered at Cheyenne, Wyoming, and living in the Inter Ocean Hotel. The city directory described his occupation as a stock inspector.[112] He must, by that time, have developed an affinity for Cheyenne, as he was periodically headquartered there since 1878 when he was a Union Pacific detective. Coincidently, in the same city directory, one Anne Smith is listed as a servant and living nearby at the corner of Nineteenth and Evans Streets. There is no further indication that this woman might have been the wife that Smith divorced on November 9, 1885, but marital difficulties may be the reason they were living apart.

Livestock ranching had become a major economic and political force in Wyoming and Western Nebraska and by 1880 over a half-million head of cattle grazed there. This industry guaranteed a sizable income for the railroads and stockyards. Omaha and Kansas City were the principal processing centers and on any day over one-hundred acres of their holding yards could be found completely covered with cattle.

Cheyenne became a center for cattle ranchers and the town attracted many wealthy investors from Europe and the eastern states. They brought to this frontier community their customs, attitudes and lifestyles. The Cheyenne Club was created to satisfy their need to socialize in a business atmosphere that was appropriate to their culture. They built a lavishly furnished structure with a large dining, billiards and card room. The Wyoming Stock Growers Association, formed in 1873, eventually used this club as their headquarters. To protect their interests a policing arm was formed and stock inspectors were employed. These men were usually referred to as range or stock detectives. Ranchers in Western Nebraska joined the Wyoming Stock Growers Association and Whispering Smith was often assigned across the state line in the Fort Robinson and Chadron area.

Stock detectives sometimes operated outside the law but usually sought to supplement local sheriffs. Toward that end they were often deputized or commissioned as peace officers and even granted interstate authority. In

Wyoming the relationships between the cattlemen's associations and the state legislature were so close that the state paid most of the detective's salary. The typical wages paid stock detectives ranged from $100 to $150 per month in addition to expenses. By comparison, in this era a United States Deputy Marshal was paid about thirty-five dollars per month.[113]

The duties of stock detectives were many and varied. Often they were stationed at stockyards to observe market cattle. Such activities in Montana resulted in the arrest of forty-three thieves in one year. Other duties included transporting ranch payrolls, detecting settlers that kill cattle to protect crops or for food, inspecting records of butchers or meat-cutters and discouraging ranch hands from possession of brand altering devices.

Farmers and homesteaders feared visits by roving stock detectives that inspected for stolen or butchered cattle without need of warrant or other legal authority. Violations were severely dealt with, often by extra-legal means. The custom of displaying the hide of a slaughtered beef on the farm gate originated in the era. The inspecting detective could see the brand at a glance and if no theft was apparent might not further search the property.

Suppression of cattle rustling was probably the most important task in the early years of the cattlemen's association activities. Stock detectives followed suspected thieves in order to catch them in the act. Holding pastures were inspected or placed under surveillance. Visits were made to "Hog Ranches," a term used to describe crude saloons and whorehouses scattered along the trails from Laramie to the Black Hills, to identify possible rustlers loitering there.[114] Arrested thieves were charged in local courts but when grass roots sentiment against cattle barons made convictions almost impossible, extra-legal means were employed. In Johnson County, Wyoming, of 180 indictments for cattle stealing only one conviction was obtained, and that was reduced to petty larceny.[115]

The difficulty of convicting thieves was one cause for the Johnson County War. In that confrontation over forty invading cattlemen were arrested for attempting to eliminate known rustlers in the Powder River area. Among them were a half-dozen stock detectives from the Wyoming Stock Growers Association including Scott Davis, a long-time associate of Whispering Smith.[116] There was no indication that Whispering Smith was involved and he is known to have been in Utah at that time.

In cases of aggravated rustling the thieves were often shot, hung or otherwise eliminated. Settlers had their barns and homes burned when it was found they slaughtered cattle or fenced land contrary to the cattlemen's wishes. Others left their property under threat of death. The murderous activities of Tom Horn at the end of his career illustrate the extremes of a few stock detectives. In some cases, when cattlemen's associations paid rewards for captured thieves, stock detectives resorted to entrapment for their own enrichment.[117]

Rustlers became extremely active in 1883, attacking both large and small cattlemen. Ranchers with large herds had stock detectives to take direct action against the thieves. Smaller ranchers did not have this advantage and so they formed vigilante groups. Complete lack of confidence in the courts drove both groups to the extremes of murder by lynching as well as covert assassination.[118]

Since both groups had the same objectives in the same counties and against the same rustlers, it is reasonable to assume they joined forces on occasion. It is known that some vigilantes were members of the Holt County Sheriff's posse that was involved in the February 6, 1884, lynching of Albert "Kid" Wade.[119] Based on the extra-legal methods used by some stock detectives in other situations it is probable that they were involved in some of the seven northwest Nebraska lynchings in that era. Whispering Smith was assigned to this exact area at the time but his involvement can only be imagined.

The typical week for a stock detective, however, was often routine and monotonous. Whispering Smith, in a letter to his superiors dated May 26, 1886, complained that he had declined to issue several subpoenas. They were sent to him at Chadron, Nebraska, by Thomas J. Carr, U. S. Marshal for Wyoming. Smith relates that court appearances by the named cattlemen would interfere with ranch operations. One exception was made for James Chesney, a person deemed worthless by Smith. This one subpoena was served as Smith felt it would not interfere with roundups. It seems that Chesney, known as "Whitcomb Jim," had previously been caught with a stolen horse. This piece of correspondence confirms several aspects of Whispering Smith's style. He clearly enjoyed autonomy and exercised his authority in an arbitrary manner, but was prone to brag on his wise use of discretion. A deep knowledge of the local inhabitants, vagrants and ne'er-do-wells was his forte and he was not timid about exhibiting it.[120]

One well documented major event involving Whispering Smith was a contract murder that he arranged. This involvement was meticulously researched by Murray L. Carroll for an article in a professional journal. Carroll is a well-respected researcher and author on Wyoming history. He relied heavily on the correspondence files of the Wyoming Stock Growers Association held in the Archives of the American Heritage Center at the University of Wyoming. The description of Whispering Smith's involvement in this incident is based generally on Carroll's article.[121]

When John J. Hamlin came to the Sidney area his first job was at the Redington Ranch on the Platte River. In the fall of 1880 he was hired by the Wyoming Stock Growers Association to keep track of cattle killed by Union Pacific trains. Later, in July of 1881, Hamlin was promoted to Stock Inspector and by 1883 he was assigned to the Valentine, Nebraska, area.

Johnny Smith had a small ranch near O'Neill, about one-hundred miles east of Valentine. He was Hamlin's brother-in-law but Hamlin was a wife beater and Johnny Smith hated him. On the other hand, Hamlin hated Johnny Smith who was an associate of suspected rustlers. Their animosity climaxed on December 4, 1883, when Hamlin challenged Smith to meet him just south of Valentine to settle their differences.

Johnny Smith took three of his rustling companions to the meeting and while there are several versions of what followed, it is undisputed that some of Smith's group killed Hamlin. The cause of death was attributed to a shotgun wound in the chest and three revolver shots through the head.

Nothing was done about the killing for several years until Whispering Smith learned, through his informants, that Hamlin had been killed because he had developed enough evidence to convict Johnny Smith and his friends of cattle theft. Whispering Smith prevailed on the Wyoming Stock Growers Association to demand action against the killers and the county grand jury returned an indictment. Johnny Smith and his friends fled and a $200 reward was posted for Smith as he was assumed to be the actual killer.

Hamlin and Whispering Smith had been friends since the murdered stock detective was assigned to western Nebraska and he took a very personal interest in closing the case. By June, 1886, Johnny Smith using the alias J. H. Morrell, had been traced to Nogales, Arizona, through Whispering Smith's many informants. George H.

Miles, alias George Bailey was a gambler at Nogales and was probably the main informant in the matter. Based on information from Miles, Johnny Smith was arrested by U. S. Deputy Marshal James Blade. There being no jail at Nogales, Johnny Smith was confined under guard at the International Hotel and he escaped during the unexplained absence of the deputy marshals.

Johnny Smith fled to Mexico vowing revenge against George Miles. Whispering Smith was enraged and, after having already paid Miles one-hundred dollars for information, offered him another seventy-five dollars to track Johnny Smith down and kill him. This increased expenditure was approved by the Wyoming Stock Growers Association and Miles set off for Mexico.

The Plancha de Plata Mine in Sonora, Mexico, was not far from Nogales. Miles found Johnny Smith there on July 23, 1886. Miles claims he was looking for ore prospects and rode past a cabin where a man was wearing a handkerchief over his lower face due to a toothache. Miles recognized Johnny Smith through the disguise and Smith opened fire wounding the gamblers horse. Miles returned Smith's fire hitting the him in the stomach.

The wounded Johnny Smith was attended by local miners and claimed that Miles shot first without any warning. Although fatally wounded, Johnny Smith lived long enough to give a deathbed statement that he had shot at Miles only in self-defense. Miles reported the incident to Nogales authorities on July 29, 1886, but since the killing occurred in Mexico no action was taken. He left Nogales at once and Whispering Smith insured that payment was made to him at Los Angeles, California. There is no record of what happened to the $200 reward. It probably remained unclaimed although, true to his audacious nature, Whispering Smith may have applied for it.

Whispering Smith's obituary mentioned his search of the Jackson Lake area for outlaws. While no documentation is found for this claim his involvement there is quite possible. In 1886 Stock Detective Frank Canton arrested William C. Jackson at Buffalo, Wyoming. Jackson, known as "Teton Jackson" frequented the Jackson Hole area and used it as a rustling hideout. Jackson Hole and Jackson Lake were prime destinations for livestock stolen in Montana and northern Wyoming. They were re-branded there, held over the winter and resold in Idaho. Posses consisting of Wyoming sheriffs and stock detectives made several raids into the Jackson Hole area. It is possible that Whispering Smith was with one of those posses and that accounts for the mention in his obituary.[122]

A series of events all but ruined the cattle industry in the winter of 1886-1887 and eventually cost Whispering Smith his job. The most devastating storm in Great Plains history swept from Canada to Texas. Cattle froze by the thousands and the grasslands were buried in snow. Some ranchers lost eighty percent of their herds and all livestock operations were suspended during the fifty degree below zero conditions. Simultaneously a market crash wiped out some ranch owners and many investors withdrew. The situation was made even worse by European absentee owners who felt no nationalistic obligation and sold off their holdings for pennies on the dollar.

Another negative factor was the Nebraska Herd Law that was enacted in 1870 to regulate the fencing of crops. It was a local option statute and the western counties did not adopt it until the late 1880s when a series of special elections was forced by the grangers. Their purpose was to protect farmlands from the damage caused by free ranging cattle even though ranching operations would be seriously impacted.

Opposition by the cattlemen was strong and Tom Sturgis, President of the Wyoming Stock Growers Association, assigned Whispering Smith to defeat the grangers' legislation.[123] Smith scoured eastern Wyoming for ranch hands, railroad workers, roustabouts and vagrants that could be persuaded to cross the Nebraska border to vote. Just what methods of persuasion Smith used is not clear but money, liquor and coercion by employing ranchers would fit the political customs of the times. It is probable that more than a few of the transient voters were persuaded by Smith's reputation for retribution. Although more than seventy-five counterfeit voters were brought over from Wyoming, Whispering Smith's efforts failed and the grangers won the election.[124]

The combination of severe weather, economic collapse, fence laws and abandonment by investors caused a dramatic retrenching of the cattle industry. By the end of 1888 the cattle kingdoms in western Nebraska were all but gone and most large herds that remained were moved to Wyoming.

The final blow came when a new Wyoming governor discontinued the salary support for livestock inspectors that had previously been allocated through the counties. Whispering Smith wrote to the Wyoming Stock Growers Association in January, 1888, that he was in financial need and offered to settle for half the salary and expenses owed him.[125] He was still active in the Whitney and Harrison areas of Nebraska that winter working independently for several ranchers in a temporary capacity. Finally, unable to continue without income from the cattlemen, Whispering Smith returned temporarily to railroad policing. He served the Northern Pacific Railway as a detective working between Bismarck and Walla Walla but was headquartered at Helena, Montana.[126]

The supposition by some that an arrest of Harry Longabaugh, known as the Sundance Kid, was made by Whispering Smith during his service as a stock detective has caused some confusion. Longabaugh was wanted for livestock theft in Montana and traced to a hideout by officers. The *Daily Yellowstone Journal* described his arrest and credited it to Deputy Sheriff Eph Davis and Stock Inspector Smith.[127] The similarity of name and title caused the identity of the Smiths to be confused. The stock detective involved in the arrest was Wilson B. Smith, a Montana

Livestock Association detective. He was closely connected with the Custer County, Montana, Sheriffs Office and was a personal friend of Deputy Davis with whom he later posed for manhunter type photographs.[128] The confusion was caused by failure of the newspaper to sufficiently identify the stock detective involved and lack of information on the whereabouts of Whispering Smith at the time.

7

UTAH

THE YEAR 1888 WAS TRANSItional for Whispering Smith. The Wyoming Stock Growers Association was in economic decline and Smith was available for other employment. The most rapidly developing mining area of Utah was to find him a visitor by the end of the year and he established residency at Castle Gate in Emery County.

Mormon farmers were the early settlers in the area that was first Emery and later became Carbon County. They established farms along the Price River and were followed by cattle ranchers that expanded out toward the Wasatch Plateau and into the Book Cliff area. During the 1880s the Denver & Rio Grande Railroad sought a route to Salt Lake City and discovered large deposits of coal in Emery County, a fuel necessary to their operation. Mining entrepreneurs flocked to develop mineral assets and by 1894 Carbon County was formed from Emery County to facilitate the coal industry.

The Denver & Rio Grande Railroad was the major transporter of ore to the industrial centers but smaller short-line railroads were needed to connect with the mines. This was an era of unregulated corporate business practices and questionable investment opportunities. Fortunes were made and lost in ventures related to mining, rail transportation and the livestock market.

On a chilly morning in October, 1888, a group of men gathered around a table in the lounge of Ogden's premiere Broom Hotel. The hotel owner, John T. McIntosh, acted as host but the man at the head of the table was obviously in charge. He was Alexander H. Swan, the famous "Cattle King" of Cheyenne and prominent member of the Wyoming Stock Growers Association. His fortunes rose and fell but he was the perpetual entrepreneur and in the late 1880s he became involved in forming a street railway service at Ogden, Utah. To the right sat his son, William R. Swan, also a prominent investor.

Seated around the table were; Robert Robinson, a successful Ogden businessman, William Bishop, a San Francisco attorney, J. J. Sullivan, F. W. LaFranz and W. R. Williams. All these men were associated with the Swans in the street railway venture. Also present were John R. Middlemiss and William VanDyke, real estate partners at

Salt Lake City. The purpose of this meeting was formation of the Emery County Railway, a short-line service connecting mines with the Denver & Rio Grande route. The incorporation document date was October 9, 1888 and it listed the subscribers.

A. H. Swan	10 Shares
Wm. VanDyke	10 Shares
J. R. Middlemiss	10 Shares
Robert Robinson	10 Shares
Wm. W. Bishop	10 Shares
W. R. Swan	10 Shares
J. J. Sullivan	10 Shares
F. W. LaFrantz	10 Shares
J. T. McIntosh	10 Shares
W. R. Williams	10 Shares[129]

Not long after the New Year Holiday relationships began to go sour between the various incorporators. Perhaps there were personality conflicts or financial manipulations but matters came to a head the first week in January, 1889. The shareholders voted to bring removal action against William VanDyke as President and John Middlemiss as Director. The Emery County Railway was soon dissolved and it was discovered that Whispering Smith had apparently been investigating John Middlemiss for several months. The results may have precipitated the new corporation's collapse. It is probable that Alexander

H. Swan, well acquainted with Smith's abilities with the Wyoming Stock Growers Association, hired him away from the Northern Pacific Railway to conduct an investigation dealing with fraud or financial manipulation.

Later that week another short-line railroad was incorporated to perform the same service that had been intended for the now defunct Emery County Railway. This new line was named the Desert Railway Company and the principal founders were John Middlemiss and William VanDyke. No other previous Emery County investors were involved and this new effort soon collapsed. No record is found of the financial manipulations involved but the tenor of the situation would indicate that there was some fleecing of the flock

In that same eventful week some of the persons entangled in these corporate machinations were involved in a confrontation that nearly ended in gunfire. The nearby area of Schofield, Utah, was ripe for mineral exploration and several of the various investors staked claims there. John T. McIntosh, owner of the Broom Hotel, along with Daniel Hammer and J. P. Sprunt, attempted to visit their claims and were blocked by John Middlemiss, Adam Paul and two others.

Paul tore down Sprunt's claim notices and declared that he had been placed in lawful possession of the property by W. R. Williams, Secretary of the Permanent Loan & Building Association. Williams was one of the original investors in the Emery County Railway. Sprunt protested in vain. Fearing that their own claims might have been usurped both Hamer and McIntosh demanded passage through Sprunt's claim to inspect the posted notices on their mineral locations. Middlemiss and two other armed men confronted them with threats of shooting if the group tried to cross Sprunt's claim, the only way into the other properties.[130]

Although they were also armed, the threatened group declined the confrontation and retreated. One wonders what would have happened if Whispering Smith had been present. The deposed group later filed a complaint against Middlemiss and his associates in the court at Price, Utah. As the case was one of charge and countercharge it was dismissed. An account of the incident that alleged a conspiracy between Williams and Middlemiss to usurp mineral claims was published in Ogden's newspaper, *The Standard*. Middlemiss charged libel and had the editor, Frank Cannon, placed under civil arrest. This action was later reduced to a $10,000 suit against the newspaper.

Relationships between the former founders of the Emery County Railway continued to deteriorate. Whispering Smith, in the course of his investigation, began to document rumors of intemperance and indebtedness on the part of Middlemiss. Ogden's Little Queen Saloon was encouraged to sue Middlemiss for his delinquent bar tab and a judgment was given against him.[131]

A few days later D. O. Rideout, an associate of the Swans, served a legal notice on Middlemiss in front of spectators. Middlemiss created a scene, called Rideout a liar and scoundrel and accused him of conspiracy with the Swans. Rideout filed criminal charges against Middlemiss for disturbing the peace by traducing to fight. Middlemiss was convicted, fined ten dollars and then posted a one-hundred dollar appeal bond. The feud between the Swan group and Middlemiss accelerated.

One of Whispering Smith's techniques seems to have been the issuing of libelous or slanderous attacks on opponents in an attempt to provoke gunplay. During the Sidney gold robbery affair his letters accusing Dennis Flannagan of grand jury tampering appeared in Nebraska newspapers. Flannagan was so enraged that he confronted Smith and was killed in the ensuing gunfight. Earlier in Cheyenne, Smith launched a slanderous denunciation against J. G. Mills. The outcome was a confrontation that almost resulted in a duel.

Whispering Smith's continuing investigation of John R. Middlemiss in the early months of 1889 led him to publish and distribute a broadside, perhaps to cause a deadly confrontation. It took the form of a bulletin to law enforcement officers. A number of alleged frauds and crimes were associated with Middlemiss and this was followed by an appeal for more information about him. The bulletin, similar to the type used by the Pinkerton Agency, was distributed to police chiefs and sheriffs as well as the general public.

Chief of Police

John R. Middlemiss, alias Capt. J. R. Middlemiss, about 40 or 50 years of age, weight about 170 or 180 pounds, about 5 feet 10 or 11 inches in height, dark complexion, black eyes, grey hair, cut short, stout build, big flat feet No. 10. At the present time he is clean shaved, excepting a small dark or artificially colored moustache which he usually wears pointed at the end, at times however he wears a large full beard heaviest on his chin, dresses well, looks genteel. It is said he kept a drug store, has been a life insurance agent and claims to be a mining expert, talks French and German, but it is believed he is a Canadian of Scots and French descent.

He has a good address with much cheek and impudence and is what is called by crooks "a smooth mug." He is much addicted to drink and when under the influence of liquor which he is about two thirds of the time, he will become engaged in saloon brawls and fisticuffs. He has operated in various parts of the world under different names, he is a good scribe and writes very rapidly, his handwriting in letters and bill is in my possession, and I am satisfied he is crooked and wanted in different localities. It is said that he is well known to Hugh Geary, and has done time with him (Geary is a confidence man in Denver and on the Pacific Coast.)

Middlemiss, like all such characters, will squander money freely when he has it, and will not hesitate to bilk hotels and run his fees in saloons when without money. In saloons he will assume all the dignity of a man with unlimited means. He will sing Scotch songs when meeting Scotchmen in saloons. He has asserted that he was a Captain in the Confederate service and has endeavored to get the Mormons to baptize him in their church, telling them that he could go south and with one speech raise an army of ten thousand and lead the children of Israel out of bondage.

He succeeded in swindling an old man here over the age of 70 out of 11 town lots the proceeds of which he surrendered, and the transaction was done in such a clever manner that I doubt very much that he can be convicted. As a mining man he is a fraud, he knows nothing theoretically or practically about mines or minerals, he has been arrested in various places on the Pacific Coast and in Canada and was arrested for embezzlement in Virginia City, Nevada, a year ago. Some years ago he skipped out of Montreal and left many creditors to morn. From his general makeup,

> *his motions and expressions, I believe he has at times in his checkered career turned to preaching in the capacity of an itinerant preacher. His asertation that he has been a Captain in the late Confederate service is not only a shameful lie, but it is an outrage and gross libel on the good people of the south.*
>
> *All officers of the law whose business it is to hunt down and bring to justice rouges, frauds and traveling bilks, are respectfully requested to furnish me with any information they have or may obtain concerning the above described character.*
>
> *Respectfully,*
> *James L. Smith. Detective*[132]

Shortly after Whispering Smith distributed this bulletin, financed by the Swans, he encountered Middlemiss on an Ogden street. Angry words were exchanged and Middlemiss accused Smith of harassment in a long string of expletives. Smith chased him into a grocery store and threw a lit cigar in his face. If this was an attempt to trigger gunplay it failed and Middlemiss, instead of reacting as had Flannagan and Mills in the past, fled and lodged a complaint with authorities. Charges of criminal libel were brought against Smith. An indictment was found against him and the case was set for trial on May 28, 1890. Bail was set at

$2,000 and posted by John T. McIntosh, W. R. Swan and R. Robinson, all original Emery County Railway investors.

At trial, Smith's attorney presented a strong case for the defense but in the time available he was unable to obtain the witnesses needed to substantiate the allegations made in Smith's bulletin. As most of Smith's information came from distant sources, slow mail and travel expenses prevented its use as evidence. Whispering Smith was found guilty by the jury and the court fined him $300 but the judge suggested an appeal to the Supreme Court.[133] There is no record of an appeal and it may be that Smith's attorney felt that it would be less costly to accept the miniscule fine than to pursue the matter, particularly if the Swans were paying it.

An interesting article appeared in an Ogden newspaper indicating that Middlemiss was generally thought to be a rogue. The lead sentence was, "Captain James L. Smith is in town. He is the gentleman that hunted down Captain J. R. Middlemiss to his hole more than once."[134] The wording of the article would indicate that public opinion favored Smith over Middlemiss in their recent controversy and that Middlemiss was thought to be less than honorable.

John Middlemiss soon left the Ogden area but continued his prospecting activities in the Skull Valley district of Toole County, Utah. He was elected Recorder for the Mercur Mining District in 1895 and was responsible for keeping records of claims, transfers and protests. This function was soon transferred to the County Recorder raising the question...had the fox been put in charge of the chicken coop?[135]

In the years following the collapse of the cattle business and the Middlemiss affair, Whispering Smith explored other occupations. By 1891 he was prospecting for mineral deposits in Utah. Perhaps he had been bitten by the coal claim bug through his association with the Swan group. Smith was moderately successful, made several coal claims, survived a court dispute for ownership and later sold his holdings to the Pleasant Valley Coal Company.[136]

An interesting interlude in Whispering Smith's life was his fifty-third birthday party. At a social held on January 26, 1891, many of the prominent citizens of Castle Gate gathered for an evening of dancing and refreshments to celebrate his "thirty-eighth" birthday. Apparently his conviction for criminal libel had no effect on his social standing. Perhaps his encounter with Middlemiss actually increased his esteem with citizens of the mining districts. The gathering was climaxed by a roast wherein many speakers toasted Smith with a satirical treatment of his career. There was no explanation of the pun involved with the dissimilarity of birthdates except that Smith was born in 1838. It was doubtless an inside joke.

Newspaper accounts of the event commented on Smith's kind and gentlemanly demeanor and his large number of friends in the community. After the others finished toasting him, Whispering Smith commanded the floor and responded with, "Ladies and gentlemen, I will frankly admit that I can be compared to an aged tree in the forest, the branches of which have stood the storms of many years, its foliage has been withered by the scorching sun of many summers and its bark peeled of by the cold blasts of many winters, but I rejoice to know the old tree itself still stands."[137]

Discouraged or bored with prospecting and land speculation, Whispering Smith returned to his occupation as a railroad detective, but not again with the Union Pacific or Northern Pacific. Instead he served the Denver & Rio Grande Railway in Utah and Colorado.[138] He must have been surprised at the changes in railroad policing when he again became a railroad detective in the 1890s. The primary mission of the Union Pacific detectives in the 1870s was the protection of the railroad's extended business environment. Stagecoach robbery, rustling, outlaws gangs and Indian reservation problems had the highest priority.[139]

In his new position with the Denver & Rio Grande his primary duties related to internal protection. Some railroad employees were tempted to embezzle funds or steal property. The frequent train wrecks required immediate security to prevent theft of goods from freight cars. Passengers needed protection from crooked gamblers, con-men and drunks. Supporting the authority of and preventing attacks on conductors became important to railroad efficiency.

In addition, the 1890s brought the specter of aggravated labor difficulties and railroad detectives were used to suppress disturbances and recruit strike-breakers. The threat of unionization by increasing numbers of railroad and mine workers would soon consume more of the railroad detective's efforts than any of the other tasks.

Smith's employment with the Denver & Rio Grande brought him into contact with their primary Utah customer, The Pleasant Valley Coal Company, and he was eventually hired as their security officer. His 1897 appearance before the Carbon County Commissioners arose from that employment and was an attempt to protect his company from the activities of local outlaws.

Carbon County's Commission meetings were usually poorly attended but the hall was crowded on the day Whispering Smith held up his hand to stop the deliberations. The surprised commissioners set aside Sheriff Gus Donant's proposal to hire C. L. Maxwell as his deputy and turned to see who demanded the floor. They observed an impressive figure wearing a dark frock coat and whose deep-set black eyes blazed with intensity as he began to softly speak. They leaned forward to hear why this tight-lipped gentleman had interrupted their mid-April, 1897, meeting. In a quiet voice, his lips hardly moving, he introduced himself as James L. Smith and the one responsible for the protection of the Pleasant Valley Coal Company at Castle Gate, the largest business in the county.

Smith handed each commissioner a copy of a proposed resolution and fiercely attacked Sheriff Donant's attempt to hire C. L. Maxwell. Declaring Maxwell to be a thief and rustler, Smith went on to criticize Sheriff Donant's office as being corrupt and ineffective. Then he called the commissioners attention to his resolution that demanded the resignation of Sheriff Donant and demanded the appointment of an experienced replacement of good reputation. The resolution was in standard form.

> Whereas: There has been and now is within the confines of Carbon County a band of desperados who have at sundry time and places committed offenses openly and violated the laws of Carbon and the State, and Whereas: No effort has been made by the sheriff to capture said lawless band and to put an end to such lawlessness, and Whereas: It has been reported to members of the Board of County Commissioners by reputable citizens of this county that the sheriff of this county, Gus Donant, has refused and willfully neglected to perform the duties of his office as sheriff to the detriment of the best citizens and taxpayers, and to the disgrace of the county, and Whereas: The petition of Jas. L. Smith, Special Officer of the Pleasant Valley Coal Company, recites and sets forth in more tangible form the reports which have from time to time been reported

to the Board of County Commissioners; Now, therefore, be it resolved that the Sheriff of Carbon County, Gus Donant, be and is hereby requested to hand in his resignation as Sheriff of Carbon County forthwith to the end that a citizen may be appointed who will perform the duties of this office without fear or favor, that the county may regain her good name and become once more a desirable place for peaceable citizens to locate and settle and in which capital may be invested with safety. And be it further resolved: That if the sheriff refuses to resign, the County Attorney is hereby instructed to institute proceedings against him on the charges set forth in the petition of Jas. L. Smith, Special Officer of the Pleasant Valley Coal Company or any other charges which he may find evidence to sustain, It is also ordered that the County Clerk be instructed to notify the Sheriff of the above action.[140]

The seed of the problem was the state of general lawlessness in the area coupled with ineffective and corrupt law enforcement. Outlaw gangs such as the Wild Bunch hid in inaccessible retreats at Robber's Roost, Hole-In-The-Wall, and Brown's Hole and ranged throughout the area. Rustling, bank and train robbery thrived while a portion of the population that disliked cattle companies and wealthy commercial interests supported or was apathetic to such crime. Smith's fear was that, since the Carbon County mines brought payroll funds from Salt Lake City by rail, there was a great probability for robbery.

Smith was convinced that Sheriff Donant was incompetent and probably corrupt. The need to remove Donant became essential when he announced that C. L. Maxwell, alias "Gunplay" Maxwell, was to be appointed as a deputy. Maxwell, also known as John Carter, was a small time rustler in the vicinity of Nine Mile Canyon, just east of Price, Utah. He was humorously called "Gunplay" because of several confrontations where he was disarmed and humiliated before he could draw his revolver.[141] Maxwell had been an occasional member of a gang at Robber's Roost that included Butch Cassidy and Matt Warner. Somehow Maxwell befriended Sheriff Donant and promoted himself as a candidate for deputy sheriff. Maxwell apparently was unaware of Whispering Smith's ability to develop intelligence on criminal groups and the identity of their members.

After lengthy consideration Smith's resolution was adopted and Sheriff Donant was ordered to resign. Donant refused and sought legal representation. The County Attorney, J. W. Warf, was a friend of the sheriff and procrastinated enforcement of the decision.. Smith saw this as proof of political corruption in Carbon County. The following months were characterized by charges and counter-charges between Smith and Donant's several attorneys.

Concurrent with this political feud plans were under way to rob the Pleasant Valley Company Payroll. Butch Cassidy and several of his outlaw gang had hungered after that potential loot for some time. Various unsavory residents of Castle Gate kept Cassidy informed on the system used to transport the payroll. Aware of the risk, the company paid on irregular days to confuse potential robbers. The miners were notified of the payroll's arrival by the paymaster who ordered a special blast of the mine's steam whistle.[142]

About every two weeks the payroll containing gold and silver coinage originated at Salt Lake City and was brought to Castle Gate by the Denver & Rio Grande Railway. It was unloaded at the Castle Gate depot, turned over to the mine's paymaster and then hand carried about seventy yards to the Office of the Pleasant Valley Coal Company where miners had to file up the stairway to the second-story payroll windows to draw their wages. Once the special whistle signaled a payroll arrival the miners flocked to the depot area and milled around the rail yard at the foot of the stairway.

Cassidy, aware that Whispering Smith was alerted to the possibility of a robbery by the attempt to have Sheriff Donant removed, decided on a bold approach. His plan was to use only a few confederates, get as close to the loot as possible without attracting attention, then grab it and run. He chose to loiter in the village of Castle Gate until the next payroll arrived. Each day he listened for the special blast of the mine whistle and soon became a fixture at the saloon run by Frank Caffey. His partner, Elza Lay, made himself inconspicuous and waited to back Cassidy's play.[143]

Robert LeRoy Parker, alias Butch Cassidy, was a Utah native and a ranch hand turned rustler. He later became an outlaw leader at Robber's Roost. His gang soon turned to train and bank robbery. He led Elzy Lay and Bob Meeks in the robbery of a bank at Montpelier, Idaho. That successful venture on August 13, 1896, netted them over $6,000 and when it was squandered they turned their attention to the payroll bonanza
at Castle Gate.[144]

Bob Meeks, involved with Cassidy and Lay at the Montpelier bank robbery, worked with his cousin, Joe Meeks. Both men lived in Huntington, Utah, near Castle Gate. They arranged relays of horses for the gang to use in their flight from the payroll robbery. During that escape Cassidy rode a horse borrowed from Joe Meeks.[145]

Joe Walker was a known rustler in the area and an occasional partner of C. L. Maxwell. The two fell out when Maxwell informed on Walker and caused him to be pursued by a posse. Walker fled to Robber's Roost and joined Cassidy's gang. He was assigned to cut the telegraph wires during the payroll robbery.[146]

Cassidy loitered at Caffey's saloon on Wednesday, April 21, 1897, and when the mine whistle signaled the arrival of a payroll he strolled to the depot. Several mine employees carried heavy bags along the platform that was crowded with miners waiting to be paid.

Lay followed Cassidy and they drew revolvers forcing the mine employees to surrender the payroll. Then, menacing bystanders and hindered by the heavy bags, they mounted horses tethered nearby and rode toward the nearby town of Helper. Several others were seen to join them as they rode along the railroad tracks, probably Joe Walker and Joe Meeks. Frank Caffey, the saloon keeper, picked up one payroll sack that had been dropped along the tracks and returned it to the paymaster.[147] In no account of this robbery is the presence of Whispering Smith mentioned. The question remains...Where was the security officer that had previously been so concerned about the possibility of a payroll robbery?

The cut wires prevented quick notification to the surrounding communities. Eventually, Sheriff Donant, his resignation still pending, led a posse from Price. Other posses were formed at Castle Gate and Huntington. The leader of the Huntington posse was Joe Meeks, the very man who loaned Cassidy the horse he rode after the robbery! All three posses were unsuccessful and in the confusion of nightfall the Huntington and Castle Gate posses collided. Shots were fired and Joe Meeks was wounded in the leg. Pandemonium reigned.

Cassidy split the loot so that it could be carried back to Robber's Roost by different routes with the help of relay horses along the way. Elza Lay and a companion rode through Tory and Hanksville toward the hideout while Cassidy proceeded straight across the desert from Price.[148]

In the days following the robbery representatives from the Pleasant Valley Coal Company, the Denver & Rio Grande Railway, local cattle ranches affected by rustling and staff from the Utah Governor's office met to consider action against the outlaw gangs. A major problem was the expense of a campaign to penetrate outlaw strongholds and the unusual public support for the outlaws in many counties. The group made a decision to begin by gathering information on the exact identity of the outlaws and their specific hiding places, a task at which Whispering Smith excelled.[149]

The Denver & Rio Grande Railway assigned their Chief of Detectives, Cyrus W. Shores, to head the investigation as they felt some responsibility for loss of the payroll. Cyrus "Doc" Shores was a popular and efficient lawman and was previously the Sheriff of Gunnison County, Colorado. Whispering Smith was teamed with Shores and the pair began to plan their investigation. Smith was probably well known to Shores from his previous employment with the Denver & Rio Grande.

In early May, 1897, the pair confirmed that the robbery was planned with the assistance of parties in Castle Gate who were connected with or known to the Pleasant Valley Coal Company. The investigators also complained that the company was notoriously careless in handling payroll transportation and had previously been warned by Smith of the risks.[150]

Over a month later a plot was discovered for a second robbery. Frank Caffey, the saloon keeper that helped recover some of the loot on the day of the robbery, came forward with information. He alleged that on Monday, June 21, paymaster Parrott would be robbed as he arrived at nearby Helper on Denver & Rio Grande Train Number Two. The act was to be done by men named Foote and Maxwell. Foote, who lived in Helper and was well known as a petty criminal, was to be the lookout. If the payroll was with Parrott, Foote was to signal Maxwell who would commit the robbery with the help of an unknown associate.

A dummy payroll was made up and given to Parrott who agreed to participate in a dangerous scheme to trap the robbers. Smith and Shores were to be concealed nearby and their intention was to shoot the outlaws if they attempted the robbery. This decision, affirmed by the coal company and railroad, indicates the risk both detectives felt they were taking in such an encounter. When Train Number Two puffed into Helper Parrott stepped off with the dummy payroll. Foote and Maxwell were nowhere to be seen.[151]

Following this disappointment Whispering Smith suggested that he had developed a new line of investigation. He alleged that the Castle Gate saloon keeper, Frank Caffey, may have been connected with the Cassidy gang before the robbery and that some others involved were men named Fowler and Dixon. Dixon was probably Will Roberts, alias Will Dixon. Fowler's identity in uncertain but this may be an alias used by Elzy Lay or the man who rode away from the Castle Gate robbery with Lay.

Smith claimed that, while a stock detective at Chadron, Nebraska, he had known Frank Caffey whose actual name was Benjamin Franklin Caffey. Smith theorized that Will Dixon and Cassidy had gone to Chadron where a portion of the loot was deposited in a bank and where Cassidy was now hidden by friends. The trip and bank cooperation was supposed to have been facilitated by Caffey. The Pleasant Valley Coal Company decided to send Smith and Shores to Chadron, although the distrusting company manager, George W. Kramer, felt that Smith knew more about the situation than he revealed.

Kramer and Shores had been lifelong personal friends and this may be the reason he insisted that Shores accompany Smith on a trip that might involve recovery of the stolen payroll.[152] The relationship between Smith and Caffey has never been made clear but it continued the rest of Smith's life. Caffey and Foote had an ongoing business relationship in Salt Lake City for years following the robbery. The reason that Kramer distrusted Smith in this situation has not been explained.

It was arranged for Smith and Shores to take the train for Denver on Tuesday night, June 22, and then on to Chadron by connecting spur lines. The results of their investigation are yet to be found among the records of the Pleasant Valley Coal Company or the Denver & Rio Grande Railway. It should be noticed that in Whispering Smith's obituary, seventeen years later, it was claimed, "…he was the only peace officer who ever penetrated the Hole-In-The-Wall while searching for outlaws…"[153] This raises the possibility that Smith and Shores included the Hole-In-The-Wall in their journey. That hideout is located about a hundred miles west of Chadron and the trip could have been made by rail and rented horses. Experts on the Hole-In-The-Wall, however, can provide no support for this theory and have no further information on the possible trip.[154]

In the aftermath of the Castle Gate robbery the participants shared diverse fates. Gunplay Maxwell and a partner named Porter stuck up a bank at Springville near Provo, Utah. The pair stole $3,000 and bungled their escape. Porter was killed and in September, 1898, Maxwell was sentenced to an eighteen-year term. In November, 1903, his sentence was commuted for unknown reasons. Paradoxically, he was then hired as a mine guard at Castle Gate! He may have been hired to intimidate workers involved in a strike and when the labor difficulties ended he was dismissed. Maxwell remained in the Carbon County area and in 1904 became part owner of a mine in partnership with Benjamin F. Caffey and C. W. "Doc" Shores.[155] How this diverse trio came to be associated in a business enterprise after their previous involvements in the Castle Gate robbery defies explanation and fuels conspiracy theories.

Maxwell continued to be involved in violence during the next few years and was severely injured in a gunfight at Helper, Utah, in 1907. After recovering from his injuries he left Carbon County for Nevada where he was charged with a stage coach robbery at Rawhide in 1908. Once again back in Price, Utah, he quarreled with and was killed by Edward Johnson, a local deputy sheriff.[156]

Elzy Lay was involved in a July, 1899, Train robbery with the Ketchum gang. He was wounded, captured and sentenced to life imprisonment in the New Mexico Territorial Prison. Lay won parole in 1906 and was not further involved in criminal activity.

Bob Meeks was identified as one of the Montpelier bank robbers in September. 1897. He was convicted and sentenced to thirty-two years, the maximum under Idaho law. Meeks attempted an escape by jumping out a high prison window. One leg was broken and later amputated. He was then paroled because it was proposed that he could no longer be involved in crime...and he wasn't.

Joe Walker left the Wild Bunch to continue his rustling activities and he was shot to death by a posse near Thompson, Utah, in May, 1898. It was thought for a time that he was Butch Cassidy but this was later disproved when the body arrived at Price, much to the embarrassment of the posse.

Butch Cassidy and his gang continued to rob banks and trains. In 1902 he and Harry Longabaugh, alias The Sundance Kid, left for South America along with a female companion named Etta Place. Some researchers disagree but most are convinced that both outlaws were killed by Bolivian police in 1909.

Sheriff Gus Donant was finally removed from office in July, 1897, and Charles W. Allred was appointed in his place, Allred's father was the marshal at Beaver, Utah, and often used his son as a deputy. The appointment was well supported by the community and local commercial interests. The following October Sheriff Allred appointed James L. Smith as a special deputy to serve without pay. This was specifically to meet the needs of enforcement at the Pleasant Valley Coal Company.[157]

Whispering Smith continued his verbal feud with Gus Donant's attorneys, Braffet and Warf, on through the balance of 1897. This acrimony affected Smith's ability to bring coal company cases before the local court as Warf was still the county prosecutor. Smith began to drink excessively as the Christmas Holidays approached. With this intemperance he became increasingly quarrelsome.

On Christmas Day Whispering Smith became so drunk that Sheriff Allred took him to the Mathis Hotel to sleep it off. Mrs. Hart, the hotel manager, called Allred back within the hour. She claimed that Smith had insulted her and threatened her family with his revolver. The embarrassed sheriff had no alternative but to take Smith off to jail and the next day his old enemy, County Prosecutor Warf, filed charges against him. Smith was allowed to plead guilty, was fined five dollars and the judge ordered him to sober up.[158]

A few days later, on December 30, 1897, Whispering Smith entered the crowded railway depot at Price and loitered near a freight door. Attorneys Warf and Braffet turned away from the ticket window, apparently not seeing Smith, and walked out on the platform to board a waiting train. One version holds that Smith followed them, called out a challenge and drew his revolver. As he leveled his weapon both attorneys sprang aside and Smith's first shot passed between them.

Warf fled down the platform as he drew a small revolver from a coat pocket. Smith emptied his revolver at Warf but failed to hit him, raising a question as to Smiths sobriety at the time. Then Smith began to calmly reload his revolver and Warf took this opportunity to fire several shots at his adversary. Smith walked toward Warf to shorten the shooting distance. Warf fled from the depot to Brafffet's office where he knew a shotgun to be stored. Thus armed he rushed to the courthouse and swore out a complaint charging Smith with assault to commit murder.[159]

Meanwhile Sheriff Allred arrived at the depot and disarmed Smith who remained there surrounded by a spectator crowd. Both went to the courthouse where, when Warf's complaint was examined, Smith was arrested. Whispering Smith then filed a counter-complaint charging that Warf forced the encounter and fired the first shot. Both men were released on bond and Sheriff Allred was left to interview witnesses and determine what actually happened.

Smith's complaint against Warf was dismissed

during the grand jury hearings that followed but Smith was held for trial set in District Court for February 14, 1898. He was to be tried for assault with intent to commit murder. At that trial Whispering Smith managed to have the charge dismissed on technical grounds and again escaped legal responsibility for his combative nature. He alleged that it was unlawful for the prosecutor to be the principal prosecution witness.[160]

Cyrus Shores arrived in Price for the trial, probably to serve as Smith's character witness. Whispering Smith is not again mentioned in connection with the Pleasant Valley Coal Company. Perhaps this escapade, illness or his increasing use of liquor cost his position. He was, however, later rehired by the Denver & Rio Grande as a detective and this may be attributed to his friend, Cyrus Shores, who was soon to be made Chief of Police at Salt Lake City.[161]

Whispering Smith, now referred to as "Cap Smith" apparently became ill during this period and traveled several times to Salt Lake City for treatment. Nothing is known about the nature of his illness but alcoholism is a possibility. The 1900 U. S. Census for Salt Lake City lists him as an inmate of the county Infirmary.[162] His census identifying details are correct except for two details and that may be due to his condition during the enumeration interview. His identity is further confirmed by his listing at the infirmary in the 1900 Salt Lake City Directory.

8

COLORADO

A DISPUTED EPISODE IN Whispering Smith's life is his alleged attempt to kill or frighten Bat Masterson into leaving Denver at the turn of the century. Different and conflicting versions of this incident have appeared in the literature, mostly quoting the exposé driven Denver newspapers of the era.

William "Bat" Masterson, following his career as a western peace officer and gunfighter, became involved in the sport of prizefighting. He managed a number of pugilists and became well known in Denver sporting circles. A close association with gambling interests and his aggressive nature caused brawls that created a host of enemies.[163]

Denver was served by a number of newspapers and several were in fierce competition. The *Denver Post* aligned with the Republicans while the *Denver Times* favored the Democrats. Other papers split on social issues such as suffrage and prohibition. The *Denver Post* was owned by Fred Bonfils and Harry Tammen who had many differences with Bat Masterson. Their sports editor was Otto C. Floto a rotund, two-hundred-fifty pound, native Californian boxing enthusiast.

Bat Masterson and Otto Floto were drawn together by their mutual interest in pugilism. In April, 1899, they became partners in a boxing club called the Colorado Athletic Association. The partnership was short and the split generated extreme hostility between the pair that resulted in a street fight between them in July, 1900. Floto later alleged that Masterson goaded him into the fight as an attempt to generate a self-defense killing.[164]

Thus, in addition to the many other enemies generated by Masterson's combative nature, the powerful owners of the *Post*, Bonfils and Tammen, threw their support behind their stout sports editor. Competing Denver newspapers helped to fan the fire by carrying conflicting stories about each incident in the feud.

Sometime, probably late in the summer of 1900, Whispering Smith was in Denver and had an encounter with Masterson. The exact date is difficult to pinpoint and it should be noted that Smith, now age sixty-two, was probably a patient at a Salt Lake infirmary as late as

June 14, 1900. Alfred Henry Lewis, an author and admirer of Masterson, claims that Masterson learned Smith was in town to do him harm and sent a note to a prizefighter named Patrick Gallagher who was thought to have hired Smith. The note suggested a meeting to settle the matter and, when this communication became public, Smith denied that he was in Denver to make trouble.[165]

The *Post* differed in their report of the incident. They held that Masterson made slighting remarks about Smith in a saloon. Smith entered that place to demand an accounting and Masterson fled out the back door. The *Post* held that Smith left word that Masterson should leave town…and he did.[166]

Masterson, in a September, 1900, newspaper story, accused Bonfils and Tammen of hiring an assassin and suggested they should hire a better man. He added that if the *Post* did so, and if the new killer missed, Masterson would not miss either of them.[167] Shortly after the November, 1900, elections Masterson left Denver and did not return for almost two years.

Whispering Smith, in a later interview, recalls an entirely different version. He claims to have been hired as a bodyguard for two men that wanted to conduct their business on the streets of Denver without interference. These two men had a misunderstanding with Masterson and Smith later learned that the pair were blackmailers. Masterson, based on Smith's association with the pair, asserted that Smith had been hired to kill him. When that story reached Smith he sought out Masterson in a saloon. Masterson fled and Smith claims it was then that he left a message that caused Masterson's departure from Denver.[168]

In evaluating the entire episode, some coincidences should be considered. Whispering Smith may have, then or later, been in the employment of the *Denver Post*. The Denver City Directory for 1901 lists James L. Smith, living at 1862 Curtis, as a watchman for the *Denver Post*.[169] If this guard was Whispering Smith it might add some credence to Masterson's claim that Bonfils and Tammen hired Smith as an assassin. Such an arrangement would place Smith in a legitimate salaried position while he stalked Masterson.

During the period of the alleged incident between Masterson and Smith they both seem to have been habituates of the same close neighborhood. The area between Fourteenth and Nineteenth Streets and between Curtis and Larimer Streets consisted primarily of hotels, transient boarding houses, saloons, sports halls and places of assignation. Masterson's Olympic Fight Club was at Sixteenth and Larimer, his favorite saloons were Murphy's at 1617 Larimer, the Arcade at 1613 Larimer and he rented quarters at 1825 Curtis Street.[170] There was a James Smith rooming at 1862 Curtis in 1901.[171] Could Masterson and Smith have frequented the same haunts without having some contacts that were not mentioned in the assassination stories?

On Bat Masterson's return to Denver in 1902 he

went on a long drinking spree and became a major nuisance. Hamilton Armstrong, Denver's Chief of Police, arranged to have Masterson scared out of town again, much as may have been done by Whispering Smith two years before. Sheriff Jim Marshall from Cripple Creek and an old acquaintance of Masterson's, was persuaded to do the job.[172]

Masterson got word of the plot and left a challenge for Marshall to meet him, presumably for a shootout. Masterson became bored while waiting for Marshall and began drinking at a nearby saloon. Marshall entered, got the drop on Masterson and in their following conversation Masterson agreed to…and did leave Denver for the last time.[173]

Harry Tammen and the *Denver Post* were later to be involved with the Sells Foto Circus when they financed Buffalo Bill Cody in his last Wild West show attempt. Cody was in ill health and felt victimized by Tammen. In a showdown between them, Cody had two loaded revolvers on the table and threatened to kill Tammen if not released from the circus contract. Cody won but he died shortly thereafter.[174]

Following his Denver involvement with Masterson, Whispering Smith was recorded as visiting one of his old haunts, Sidney, Nebraska. On May 19, 1903, he paused there long enough to give an interview to the local newspaper. He claimed to be on a trip to Lincoln, Nebraska, for a meeting with the Governor Mickey and the paper reported that he was, "...in the employ of the stockman's secret service."[175] Nothing was included to explain the nature of Smith's business with Governor Mickey. It is probable that his employer at that time was once again the Wyoming Stock Growers Association and not the newly incorporated Nebraska Stock Growers association as they contracted with the Wyoming group for investigative services in their early years. However, it is also possible that Smith had found employment with the National Cattlemen's Beef Association that was founded in 1898 at Denver. He may have been involved in security at the Denver Stock Yards. In passing through Sidney by rail he may have begun the trip in Cheyenne or Denver and either location would correlate with employment with one or the other cattlemen's group.

A search of the Governor Mickey Collection, including his appointment calendar, failed to reveal a connection with James L. Smith nor was anything found in Nebraska newspapers. This indicates that the subject of the meeting was probably a private matter. An examination of concurrent events, an understanding of the politics of the era and knowledge of the type of services provided by Whispering Smith tempt a possible explanation.

Edward A. Cudahy was the very wealthy founder of an extensive meatpacking industry at Omaha, Nebraska. His Republican political and social involvements, including campaign contributions, would have made him well known to the Republican Governor of that state.

Patrick Crowe was a known violent criminal who once had a butcher shop that was put out of business by Cudahy. Crowe hated Cudahy and made threats against him.[176]

In the fall of 1900 Crowe and an accomplice, Jim Calahan, plotted to extract revenge on Cudahy and become rich in the process. On December 18, 1900, they kidnapped sixteen year-old Eddie Cudahy, the son of the millionaire, and demanded $25,000 in gold coin as ransom. This demand was paid and, when his son was released, Cudahy authorized a $50,000 reward for the kidnapers and hired the Pinkerton Agency to find them.

Crowe evaded capture and fled first to London and then to South Africa. Prior to leaving he wrote a taunting letter to Cudahy offering to return a portion of the ransom if all charges were dropped. Cudahy refused but now the identity of the kidnappers was confirmed and Calahan was soon arrested, tried and acquitted on a technicality. Crowe volunteered for service in the Boer War and then returned to the United States in 1903. It is certain that Cudahy was aware of Crowe's return and felt threatened. It would be reasonable for him to consult Governor Mickey for advice and assistance. The recent events between Whispering Smith and Bat Masterson had garnered considerable publicity in Colorado and Nebraska. Perhaps Governor Mickey contacted Smith in order to refer him to Cudahy.

If so, and considering Smith's reputation, perhaps Cudahy wanted Crowe to be severely threatened or terminated to insure future tranquility. No mention is made, however, of any contact with Smith in Crowe's autobiography.[177] After a crime spree that lasted several years Crowe was finally arrested and returned to Nebraska for trial. He was acquitted of the Cudahy kidnapping by a jury whose animosity toward the rich was the main factor. Smith apparently returned to Denver and lived in the Larimer Street area.

At the conclusion of whatever business Whispering Smith may have done with Governor Mickey or Edward Cudahy he had reached the age of sixty-five. This was probably a little too old to deal with the rigors faced by railroad or stock detectives. It is likely that he found employment in the Denver area in the security field until his migration to Colorado's high Rocky Mountain area near Leadville.

The State of Colorado opened a reformatory near Buena Vista in 1892. It was located at an elevation of 7,000 feet in a sparsely populated mountain area about seventy-five miles southwest of Denver. Originally intended for younger male offenders convicted of lesser crimes its population soon included older hard-core prisoners as cell space shrank at other prisons.

Whispering Smith, at age seventy-two, was employed as a guard at the Buena Vista Reformatory during 1910. The U. S. Census for that year lists him as a widower indicating that he must have maintained some contact with his former wife, Anna, or others in Louisiana.[178] The age of the other guards at that time ranged between twenty-three and forty-eight. This disparity between Smith's age and that of the other guards may indicate some special reason for his employment. Perhaps there was some influence on his behalf by his past associates or it may have been that the institution needed an enforcer with a threatening reputation.

Little is recorded of Smith's activities as a prison guard nor of the nature of the Buena Vista Reformatory but for a small institution it appears to have had a violent record. Buried in Mount Olivet Cemetery, near the prison, are two prisoners that were shot during escape attempts.[179] These shootings occurred during the 1911-1912 era shortly after Smith left his employment as a guard.

In April, 1911, Thurman Ballard and three other prisoners ran from a work party that was supervised by an armed guard. Two were captured by a local farmer but the other two fled across a small river. The guard, Elmer Hawkins, fired his rifle at them and hit Thurman Ballard in the arm and leg. Ballard later died of his wounds and was buried in the Mount Olivet Cemetery. This shooting indicates that it was prison policy to use deadly force to stop fleeing convicts.

There is a possibility that the aging Whispering Smith, although no longer employed as a guard, was involved in the second shooting. Three prisoners escaped from the reformatory on July 18, 1912. Two fled into the mountains and were pursued with bloodhounds. The third, Stephen Marko, apparently made his way toward Leadville. He was known to have had a brother and a girlfriend there. Prison authorities considered him dangerous and immediately posted a fifty-dollar reward.

The residents of Bucktown, just south of Leadville, viewed a dramatic incident on the afternoon of July 19. Witnesses related that they saw two men walking up a road. One was an old man that was holding the arm of the other, a young man. Suddenly the younger man pulled free and ran toward a honeycomb of shacks. The aged man drew a revolver, rested it across his forearm and fired three shots. One shot struck the fleeing young man in the head and he fell to the ground. The shooter calmly walked away and disappeared.[180]

A mystery developed when neither the shooter nor the deceased could be identified. It took several days before all the witnesses that had seen the pair at various locations could tell their story. A search was launched for the shooter who was described as a mustached older man wearing a grey coat and a light colored soft brimmed hat. He was never located according to the newspaper reports. Several days later the victim was identified as the escapee, Stephen Marko. Witnesses felt that the actions of the elderly man indicated that he had Marko in custody and was marching him toward Leadville.[181]

Marko's body was returned to the reformatory and later buried in the prisoner's section of Mount Olivet Cemetery where their records state that he was shot to death in Leadville by a prison guard.[182] The administration of the Buena Vista facility can provide no further information. The fact that that cemetery records list the shooter as a guard, that he disappeared after the shooting instead of remaining with the prisoner, that the witnesses claim the shooter was an older man coupled with the shooter's desire to avoid identification add to the possibility that he was Whispering Smith. The essence of the man permeates the incident.

This theory about Marko's death is based on Smith's past involvements, scruples, temperament and the circumstances of the situation. Whispering Smith was renowned for his ability to develop informants, mingle with criminals and learn details of their background. His tour as a guard lasted from May, 1909, to May 10, 1910. Marko's first term at Buena Vista ended on April 4, 1910. Thus Marko and Smith were probably known to each other for at least a year. Guards learn a great deal about prisoners when supervising them at work. They are often involved in conversations about families, past misadventures and future hopes.

When Smith resigned in 1910 he likely returned to Denver and again resided in one of the resident hotels or rooming houses in the Larimer Street district that he frequented off and on from 1900 until his death. A community telephone was, by then, commonly found in the lobby of such buildings. The news of Marko's escape could have reached Smith before noon on July 18, 1912. It may have come from one of the informants he cultivated in the Chaffee County area, former friends at the prison or past

Buena Vista drinking companions.

    Once informed of the escape, Smith may have been motivated to respond. Perhaps he saw an opportunity to refresh his reputation as a man-hunter or prove that he was not just an over-the-hill lawman. The fifty-dollar reward may have been an added stimulus. While a paltry sum today, it was a whole month's pay for a guard at Buena Vista in 1912. If Smith boarded a train at Denver in the early afternoon he could have covered the seventy miles to Pueblo in a few hours. The rail net would then have taken him through Salida and Buena Vista placing him at the Malta rail yard that evening. Smith was very adept at rail travel and may even have kept a pass from his former Denver & Rio Grande employment as a detective.

    Whispering Smith, using his knowledge of Marko's past and relatives living in the Stringtown and Malta area, probably set up surveillance and waited for results. Marko was familiar with the area having been sentenced to prison twice from Chaffee County and he was previously a section hand for the Denver & Rio Grande. He was able to walk up the Arkansas River valley along the railroad tracks without being seen. Early on the morning of July 19 Marko burglarized a railway building at Kobe and stole a section hands clothing to replace his prison garb. He then continued north toward Malta.

    Smith probably apprehended Marko in the Malta area and started to walk him north along the railroad tracks. Deputy Sheriff Timothy Gorman claims he met the pair along the tracks near Malta. He was stationed there to watch for the escaped convicts but he failed to recognize Marko. Gorman claimed that the younger man said nothing but that the older companion told him they had been camped near Granite the night before. Gorman did not delay the pair and they continued north along the tracks.[183] It is likely that Smith did not surrender his prisoner to Deputy Gorman at this time because he was afraid of compromising the reward. He probably wanted to turn Marko in at the Lake County Jail in Leadville to insure the chain of custody and avoid having to share the reward or credit for the capture.

Smith and his prisoner continued to move through Bucktown and Stringtown on their way to Leadville, now just three miles away. It was shortly thereafter that Marko broke away from Smith and fled. Smith, then seventy-four years of age and rheumatic, was unable to pursue Marko. It was probably instinctive for him to fall back on his past solution to such problems and simply shoot the escapee. Afterward, realizing that the reward was nullified and fearing the trouble his action would cause, Smith just faded away to Denver. Prison authorities may have later learned the shooters identity but did not reveal this information as it might be an embarrassment. They did, however, record the shooter as an unnamed prison guard, perhaps to maintain a measure of correctness.

9

END OF THE TRAIL

OLD, DESTITUTE AND BROKEN in health, Whispering Smith faced a bleak fate in his final days. His solitary nature denied him the comfort of close friendships and his pride resisted all charity but welfare housing. Following his tour as a guard at Buena Vista Reformatory, Smith existed in the Denver boarding houses and transient hotels on Larimer and Curtis Streets. His divorced wife predeceased him in 1906 and he had no known relatives. These were the conditions in late July, 1914, that caused him to falsely claim responsibility for a federal bootlegging offense. His intention was to become a prisoner of the United States Internal revenue authorities in order to access custodial food, shelter and medical aid.[184]

Smith was lodged in the Denver County Jail and asked that B. F. Caffey of Salt Lake City be notified with a request for assistance.[185] Why, from all the prominent and influential men that Smith had known over his career, would he call on B. F. Caffey for assistance? It will be recalled that Benjamin Franklin Caffey owned the Magnolia Hall Saloon in Castle Gate at the time of the Pleasant Valley Coal Company robbery. That Whispering Smith would request Caffey's help opens a plethora of unexplained coincidences.

B. F. Caffey sold his Castle Gate saloon in 1900 and moved to Salt Lake City although he continued to have business interests in Carbon County. Charles Kelly, in his *The Outlaw Trail*, identifies Caffey as the old-time mining speculator involved in the Castle Gate affair and still alive at Salt Lake City in 1938.[186] The coincidences deepen when the Salt Lake City Business Directory is examined. In 1900 Caffey is listed as owning a saloon and billiard hall in partnership with J. W. Foote. It will be recalled that in the aftermath of the Castle Gate robbery a man named Foote was rumored by Caffey to be an associate of Gunplay Maxwell and part of a planned second payroll robbery. Foote's full name was not recorded in the account. There was a John W. Foote, born in 1869 and raised near Price, Utah.[187] A Salt Lake directory lists John W. Foote, age 31. saloonkeeper, at the same address as Caffey's saloon.[188] Was there some connection between Smith and these men that spanned seventeen years? Was some debt owed Smith that related to the Castle Gate robbery? Was it a debt related to insuring Smith's silence about some of those involved in the affair? Was it just coincidence that Butch Cassidy and Elzy Lay loitered in Caffey's Magnolia Hall Saloon while waiting to rob the Pleasant Valley Coal Company payroll? In any event, Smith's appeal for help apparently went unanswered by Caffey.

Benjamin F. Caffey's brother, Doctor William P. Caffey, was the first physician in practice at Castle Gate and was the company doctor for the Pleasant Valley Coal Company. Ill and seriously injured employees from the mines were treated and then transferred by train to Salt Lake City. Doctor Caffey had the authority to admit patients at the Salt Lake County Infirmary.[189] It will be recalled that Whispering Smith was a patient at that institution at the end of his employment with the Pleasant Valley Coal Company in 1900. Did Doctor Caffey have a role in treating Smith's illness or alcoholism and was it in some way connected with the other coincidences? Did the Caffey brothers fear that Smith might, in a drunken state, reveal some secrets? Did they have other than a humanitarian motive in sending him away to dry out? Perhaps the truth will only be unraveled by some future conspiracy theorist.

Whispering Smith, in a depressed state, attempted to commit suicide in his jail cell by cutting his throat with a razor during mid-August, 1914. He was treated at Denver's Mercy Hospital and returned to the Denver County Jail but he was still intent on ending his life. In late August he was able to obtain a can of lye kept in the cellblock for sanitary purposes. He mixed it with water, consumed the entire can and, although in great pain, forced himself to huddle quietly in order to avoid notice by the guards.[190] Records of Smith's arrest and incarceration are all but nonexistent. Only the inmate booking ledger was preserved and it indicates that Smith was committed to the Denver County Jail previously for eight days and that he died on the twenty-fifth day of his present term of imprisonment. When finally found by jailers he was again taken to Mercy Hospital where he died on August 27, 1914.

His body was removed to the Orahood and Davidson Funeral Parlor where it lay unclaimed. Services were conducted by those undertakers and Whispering Smith was interred at the Riverside Cemetery in Denver. He lies in Section 2, Lot 205, Block 12. Riverside Cemetery overlooks the Platte River and is the burial site for many of old Denver's famous residents as well as orphans and the impoverished.[191]

The obituaries for James L. Smith were based, for the most part, on the tales he had previously told reporters during the Bat Masterson affair. Additional information was probably gathered from the saloons and boarding houses in the Larimer district where he spent his last years. Although distorted by his braggadocio and memory lapse the material did provide valuable clues to his past. Perhaps the most informative although partly erroneous obituary appeared in Denver's *Rocky Mountain News*.

NOTED DUELIST
SUICIDE IN JAIL

Captain J. L. Smith, Gunfighter feared by "Bad Men."
Swallows Lye.

WAS FAMOUS AS DEAD SHOT

Clashed With "Bat" Masterson in
Denver Streets and Later Never
Returned to Denver.

Fortune gone, broken in health, Capt. J. L. Smith, aged 72, gunfighter, duelist and former chief of detectives for the Union Pacific railroad, who bore the distinction of being the only peace officer who ever penetrated the Hole-In-The-Wall and Jackson Lake countries in Wyoming after outlaws and escaped with his life, committed suicide yesterday afternoon by drinking lye in the county jail.

A month ago, Smith, to obtain food and shelter, according to the jail officials, surrendered himself to the federal authorities and confessed to bootlegging in Boulder County. Two weeks later he made an unsuccessful attempt to end his life by slashing his throat with a razor. The weapon was taken from him before he injured himself seriously.

Gets Hold of Lye

The lye, which he took this afternoon, was kept in the jail for sanitary purposes. He got possession of it while a guard's back was turned.

Smith was one of the most famous gunfighters of the old South. His pistol duel with Larry Boyle of Balmoral, a noted Australian gambler, on the Belle of Memphis, a star Mississippi steamboat, immediately before the war is among the rivers historic incidents. After the war Smith was chief of detectives in New Orleans and made a record there for ten years.

His fame as a sleuth and dead shot spread over the country and as a result the Union Pacific road made him chief of its detective force forty years ago. He held that position until fifteen years ago, and during most of that time he operated in the West, Cheyenne and Denver being his headquarters. He ran to earth numerous stage robbers and risked his life repeatedly in the Hole-In-The-Wall country and the Jackson's Lake territory.

Ran Masterson Out

Captain Smith achieved further fame when he encountered "Bat" Masterson in Denver, in 1899. He encountered Masterson in front of the Tabor Opera House bar and pursued him to Tom Mulqueen's place, located opposite the present site of the Joslin store. Mulqueen told Masterson who his pursuer was. The next day "Bat" left Denver and never returned.[192]

The *Denver Post*, a newspaper that had a past relationship with Whispering Smith published a shorter obituary than ran in the *Rocky Mountain News* and provided much the same information, some erroneous, some factual. It did, however, include information from the Denver County Jail Warden, John Kenney.

CAPTAIN SMITH, 72,
NOTED GUN FIGHTER
ENDS BROKEN LIFE

Dose of Lye Swallowed in
County Jail Federal Ward
Is Fatal

"Capt." J. L. Smith, 72, famous as a gunfighter in the pioneer days of the West and South, died at Mercy Hospital last night from the effects of a dose of lye taken with suicidal intent in the federal ward of the county jail where he was held to await trial on a charge of bootlegging in Boulder County.

According to Warden John Kenney, he obtained the lye while the guard's back was turned, mixed it with water and drank it. He had been possessed of a suicidal mania for more than two years and had made several unsuccessful attempts to end his life.

"He was discouraged," said Kenney. "In his lifetime he faced death at the hands of men time and time again, but he couldn't bear the idea of living out a dreary old age, with nothing to look forward to but poverty and sickness. He was broken in spirit, broken physically and 'broke' financially."

Smith was a native of the South. While yet a "kid" in years he earned a reputation as a gunfighter. Soon after the Civil War ended he became chief of detectives in New Orleans. He served in that capacity for ten years and then became chief special agent for the Union Pacific road, with headquarters in Denver and Cheyenne. He held the position until fifteen years ago earning a reputation as the only peace officer who ever penetrated the Hole-In-The-Wall country in Wyoming in search of outlaws, and came out alive.

He is generally accredited with being the man who caused "Bat" Masterson to take up his residence outside of Denver. In 1899, according to the story, Masterson made some slighting remarks about Smith in a downtown saloon. Smith entered the place and to demand an accounting and Masterson went out through the rear door. Smith followed him to another saloon and the same performance was repeated.

Tired of playing hide-and-seek with Masterson, Smith left word at several of "Batt's" haunts that he had better leave Denver. Masterson left Denver the following day and hasn't been back since.

As far as the authorities have been able to ascertain, Smith had no relatives. His burial will probably be arranged by friends.[193]

A third obituary was published in Utah about a month later. Probably some person that was aware of Smith's ten-year stay in Carbon Canyon and was in Denver at the time of Smith's death wrote back about the incident and there was a delay in editorial follow up. Void of the sensational hype presented by the other two newspapers this obituary concentrated on his known Carbon Canyon escapades. It also took a jibe at the *Denver Post*, its owners and at a local unnamed newspaper.

"CAP" SMITH PASSES

Old Timer In Carbon County Takes
His Own Life at Denver

Private advices to The Advocate state that Capt. James L. Smith, an old time resident of Carbon County, committed suicide in Denver a few days ago. Captain Smith, at the time of his death, was nearly 80 years of age, and during the past several years has lived in and out of charitable institutions.

He came to Castle Gate about 1890, and was one of the first coal claimants in that camp. He subsequently sold his holdings to the Pleasant Valley Coal Company and moved away. He afterwards returned to Carbon County as special agent for the Denver & Rio Grande interests in 1896 and 1897.

He was a polished Southern gentleman, but ever ready to fight a duel with anyone he deemed worthy of a challenge, and during his last trip to Carbon County was party to a spectacular duel with revolvers in front of the old Denver & Rio Grande passenger station.

On leaving Price Captain Smith for a time bodyguarded the two blackmailing proprietors of the *Denver Post*, which organ has furnished a prototype in Price newspaperdom.

For several years the captain had been in failing health. He left no known relatives.[194]

ADDENDUM

THE COMMONALITY OF THE Smith surname and the existence of too many James L Smiths complicate research now and probably created frustration for him during his lifetime. Smith was sure to be pleased at anything that differentiated him from others with that surname. The nickname "Whispering" and the pseudo-title "Captain" may have satisfied that need. Whispering Smith is not known to have ever personally used his nickname although others referred to him by it. He is only twice known to have used his middle name, once as Louis and once as Lewis. For the most part he is found in records as James L. Smith, J. L. Smith and Jas. L. Smith. After the mid-1880s he was often referred to as Captain Smith or "Cap." Smith.

Mention of him as a captain caused some researchers to believe the title was related to prior military rank. That has not been verified and another source for this title is just as likely. In Smith's era, men of responsibility in the protective and transportation occupations were often given the honorary title of captain. For example, the Pleasant Valley Coal Company, in its official correspondence, referred to Captain Colton and Captain Smith. Agents of Indian Reservations were commonly addressed as "Major" even though they were civilians without military background. In the Old South, men of position or property and auctioneers were often called "Colonel." The honorary title "Professor" was frequently bestowed on one-room school teachers, music instructors and proprietors of medicine shows.

It is not known just when the nickname "Whispering" was first applied to James L. Smith. He apparently had a very soft voice and a Southern accent. Julia McGillycuddy wrote that when Smith was visiting the Pine Ridge Indian Reservation she observed that his voice was gentle and she referred to him as Whispering Smith.[195] Grant Shumway, a respected Nebraska researcher, interviewed John M. Thurston, an attorney on a case investigated by Smith. Thurston claimed that Smith would not converse in a normal setting. Their nightly meetings were held in isolated locations and Smith would speak in a low tone or whisper.[196] Perhaps the nickname originated in this period.

Historian Agnes Wright Spring, in describing events along the Deadwood stage route, identifies James L. Smith as the Whispering Smith involved with the Lame Johnny lynching.[197] Doug Engebretson in his *Empty Saddles, Forgotten Names,* further identifies Whispering Smith as a Union Pacific detective, Laramie deputy sheriff and stock detective.[198] Harris, writing for *The Teepee Book*, notes that "Hawkbill" was another nickname for James L. Smith. While none called him so to his face, his beak was held to be the feature that identified him to early settlers along the Niobrara River in Nebraska.[199]

No photographs of Smith have been found and the only description of his physiognomy is provided by Edgar Beecher Bronson. While given to some inaccuracies and hyperbolic excesses his characterization includes, "…great burning black eyes, glowering deadly menace from cavernous sockets of extraordinary depth, were set in a colossal grim face, his straight, thin lipped mouth never showed teeth, his heavy tight-curling black mustache and stiff black imperial always had the appearance of holding the under lip closely glued to the upper.[200] Bronson's use of the word "imperial" indicates a goatee type beard. This was a pointed tuft on the front of the chin and was named after the Emperor Louis Napoleon III who made it popular with gentlemen worldwide. It was particularly fashionable with Southern gentlemen.

Following the 1900 affair with Bat Masterson in Denver, Smith was interviewed by the *Denver Times*.

A staff artist took this opportunity to sketch him in an office setting.[201] This sketch and Bronson's description were furnished to a professional police artist specializing in forensic illustration and the result was an image of Whispering Smith at mid-life.

Little was found as to Smith's exact physique. While there seems to be no mention of his height and weight, Bronson wrote that he, "...had a tremendous breath of shoulders and depth of chest; he was big boned, lean loined, quick and furtive of movement as a panther."[202] Denver jail inmate records do not contain a physical description but Smith must have been a man of substantial proportions else he could not have met the challenge of railroad policing that often involved a tussle with recalcitrant railroad section hands and hobos.

Comments about Whispering Smith's character and personality are conflicting. Shumway quotes Colonel A. B. Persinger as claiming that Smith was not a hero as portrayed in Spearman's book, but rather more an outlaw that provoked opponents into a fight to provide a self-defense reason for murder. Persinger owned the Hardscrabble Ranch near Lodgepole and was a resident of Sidney, Nebraska, at the time of several of Smith's gunfights in that town.[203]

Bronson held that Smith was devoid of vices, lacked a sense of humor and cultivated no immediate friends. Julia McGillycuddy wrote, "Whispering Smith's appearance suggested nothing of the 'Wild West.' His voice was gentle; he never indulged in liquor; he was not a quarrelsome man."[204] Her observation is confusing in view of Smith's later record of intemperance and bellicose encounters. Perhaps he was on his best behavior when visiting the McGillycuddy family.

Whispering Smith's education is subject to supposition. If he was employed as an engineer on steam vessels he may have acquired some knowledge of physics and mechanics by apprenticeship as a youth or later employment experience. As to his writing skills, samples from Wyoming Stock Growers Association correspondence show excellent sentence structure and organization. This could have been the result of a demanding grammar school education available in his early years or a skill developed later through the abundance of report writing required by his career. An exception was his broadside on Middlemiss that was poorly written and not typical of his other composition. Perhaps he was in his cups at the time.

Smith's religious preference was probably Protestant. New Orleans Archdiocese records indicate that his bride, Anna Mannion, was a widow and that a dispensation was granted for a mixed religion marriage. Anna was born in Ireland and if it is assumed that she was Catholic then James L. Smith was probably Protestant.

Several observations have been made on Smith's armament. Bronson claims he loved nothing but his guns and lavished great affection on them. One was a full-length forty-five that he carried in a shoulder holster and the other was a forty-five that had the barrel cut to two inches. He carried this short model in the deep side pocket of his long sack coat. On occasion he fired that revolver through this pocket.[205] Another source indicates, in at least one 1879 shooting, he used a forty-five Webley revolver.[206] If the make and caliber were accurately reported this was probably the Webley R.I.C. Model that was popular with some on the frontier. Such British revolvers were available in America from about 1875.

The sack coat mentioned by Bronson was commonly worn by business and professional men in this era. It could be single or double-breasted, was usually black and came to just above the knee. The coat was usually worn over a white shirt with a black bow or string tie. A vest was optional and was often worn just to support a watch and chain or to provide extra pockets.

The question as to Whispering Smith's deadly scoreboard is impossible to answer because of the sub-rosa nature of his activities, particularly as a stock detective. A number of suspected rustlers, homesteaders and vagrant ranch hands simply disappeared in the area served by the Wyoming Stock Growers Association. Bronson claimed, "...enough dead outlaws, thirty odd, to start, if not a respectable, at least, a fair sized graveyard."[207] This inflated estimate should be viewed with skepticism when compared to known incidents.

Whispering Smith's killing of Dennis Flannagan at Sidney is well documented. Also of record but less well documented is his killing of the Apaches, Give-Me-A-Horse and Carpio in New Mexico. It is also possible that he killed Stephen Marko in Colorado and Munson Alexander in New Orleans. His involvement in the lynching of Lame Johnny and John MacDonald is probable but his role in the hanging of Billy Mansfield and Archie McLaughlin may only be published rumor. The conspiracy to have Johnny Smith murdered in Mexico is well documented but it was not actually by Smith's hand. This total falls somewhat short of thirty.

Of course there were shooting scrapes with no fatalities. Whispering Smith tried to kill Patsy Walters and thought that he had, but Walters recovered from the wound. It is clear that Smith tried to kill the two attorneys, Warf and Braffet, but in the exchange he missed them both.

Whispering Smith's proclivity for hanging those he suspected of criminal activity arouses curiosity. Beginning in 1878 with the hanging of Bill Mansfield and Archie McLaughlin, Smith was linked by rumor, coincidence and reputation with the lynching or attempted lynching of at least five men. His role, if any, in the seven unsolved northwest Nebraska lynchings during his employment with the Wyoming Stock Growers Association remains unknown. Lynching Negroes in Louisiana during the reconstruction period was a common occurrence. If Smith was a plantation inspector for the Freedmen's Bureau he probably observed or investigated the hanging of former slaves. Perhaps this conditioned him to the technique.

The practice of dueling became obsolete as the Civil War ended but Whispering Smith seems to have had a fixation on the custom. His first known duel was purportedly with Larry Boyle just prior to the Civil War. Most of his subsequent gunfights were too spontaneous to be considered duels, yet he seems to have made a few challenges. His confrontation with Mills in Cheyenne is one example and another occurred in New Mexico.

Harris, in his memoirs, reports that Whispering Smith encountered Sheriff Pat Garrett while investigating some Mescalero Apache mischief. Smith tried to banter Garrett into a duel but the Sheriff misunderstood Smith's intent. This misunderstanding was caused by Smith's exaggerated politeness and Chesterfieldian manner. When Garrett later learned of Smith's intent he was chagrined but did not seek Smith out to carry the matter further.[208]

Parallels between James L. Smith and Alan Ladd, the actor that portrayed Whispering Smith in the popular 1948 film, are inescapable. Ladd had a successful career until midlife when his fortunes and health began to wane. He began to fear old age and loss of his good looks. By 1962 Ladd had not appeared in a film for over two years, was troubled by a liver ailment and had become alcoholic.[209]

Smith, once in demand as a detective and security officer, was reduced to employment as a bodyguard and prison guard as he aged. His health began to deteriorate and frequent mention of his excessive drinking indicates he was alcoholic.

In November, 1962, Ladd shot himself in the chest with a thirty-eight caliber revolver. Surgeons barely saved his life and the studio press touted the "accident while cleaning a gun" excuse.[210] Later, in January, 1964, Ladd was found dead at his Palm Springs, California, residence. The cause of death was announced as accidental and caused by interaction of prescribed drugs and alcohol. Some close friends felt it was suicide.[211]

James L. Smith, destitute, alcoholic and in ill health, attempted suicide by cutting his throat and then succeeded by swallowing lye in his jail cell. The coincidences in their latter years and the deaths of these two men, one who lived a dangerous life of adventure and the other who portrayed it o the screen, are undeniable.

NOTES

CHAPTER 1

1 *Los Angles Times*, March 1, 1925.
2 Jack Barefield, "Whispering Smith Rides Again," *The Railroadiana Express*, (Spring, 1997).
3 The list includes: *Whispering Smith*, 1916, Silent, Photo-Play Productions; *Whispering Smith*, 1926, Silent, Metropolitan Films; *Whispering Smith Rides*, 1927, Silent Serial, Universal Studios; *Whispering Smith Speaks*, 1935, Fox Studios; *Whispering Smith*, 1948, Paramount Studios; *Whispering Smith Hits London*, 1951, RKO; and *Whispering Smith*, 1961, Television Serial, NBC.
4 Paul O'Neil, *The End and the Myth* (Alexandria, VA: Time Life Books, 1979) 202- 203.
5 Frank H. Spearman, *Whispering Smith* (New York: Grosset & Dunlap, 1906).

CHAPTER 2

6 City of New Orleans, 4th Municipal Police Court, Case 841, November 13, 1875.
7 U. S. Census, 1880, Wyoming, Laramie, Cheyenne, 186D.
8 New Orleans Parish Recorder, Marriage Record, Book 4, Folio 272.
9 Anne Arundel County Court Marriage Licenses, Maryland State Archives, CR 49, 158-2, MSA No. CM 95-2, 63, Line 10.
10 U. S. Census, 1840, Maryland, Anne Arundel County, District 1. 119.
11 U. S. Census, 1860, Maryland, Baltimore City, First Ward. 220.
12 U. S. Census, 1870, Maryland, Baltimore City, Thirteenth Ward. 66.
13 U. S. Census, 1850, Delaware, New Castle County, Wilmington. 146.
14 Edgar Beecher Bronson, *The Red Blooded Heroes of the Frontier* (New York: George H. Doran Company, 1910), 77.
15 Union military records held by the National Archives are primarily service records and pension applications. The service records contain information on assignments, promotions, campaigns,

and other organizational matters but they usually provide little genealogical or identifying information such as place and date of birth. Pension applications, however, are rich in identifying details. A professional researcher examined both types of records for James L. Smith, born in Maryland about 1838. Those two details are the only known determinants for documenting Smith's service and no match was found.

16 *Denver Rocky Mountain News*, August 27, 1914.
17 U. S. Census, 1860, Ohio, Hamilton, Cincinnati, Ward 4. 259.
18 Carl Jones, riverboat historian, e-mail to author, August 4, 2004.
19 J. Winston Coleman, Jr., *Famous Kentucky Duels* (Lexington, KY: Henry Clay Press, 1969), pix.
20 Civil War, Records of Volunteer Officers, National Records & Archives Administration, Vol. B. 7, 13.
21 United States Naval Records Office, *Official Records of the Union and Confederate Navies in the War of the Rebellion*, Vol. 25. 280-291.
22 Cheryl Schnirring, Curator of Manuscripts, Illinois State Historical Library, e-mail to author, February 18, 2004.
23 In a further effort to confirm the identity of First Assistant Engineer James L. Smith a handwriting comparison was attempted. Known letters written by Whispering Smith in 1886 were compared to the 1862 enlistment application and 1864 resignation of First Assistant Engineer James L. Smith. Although there were several similarities the results were inconclusive. Changes in style probably occurred over the twenty-two years between the documents. Definite conclusions by a handwriting examiner are also made difficult when the samples are not directed writing. It is unfortunate that no pension application could be found for Smith as that would have confirmed his identity.

CHAPTER 3

24 Donald G. Newman, *To Set The Law In Motion: The Freedmen's Bureau and the Legal Rights of Blacks 1865-1868* (New York: KTO Press, 1979). 11-14, 72.
25 Brigadier General Samuel Thomas, Headquarters, Bureau of Refugees, Freedmen and Abandoned Lands, State of Louisiana, Correspondence, March 9, 1867.

26 Howard A. White, *The Freedmen's Bureau in Louisiana* (Baton Rouge: LSU Press, 1990), 35.
27 Roster of Civilians Employed as Assistants, Agents and Inspectors by Thomas Conway, Assistant Commissioner, National Archives Microfilm M1027, Roll 34.
28 *Denver Rocky Mountain News*, August 27, 1914.
29 Edwards 1873 New Orleans Directory. 409.
30 Dennis C. Rousey, *Policing The Southern City: New Orleans, 1805-1889*, (Baton Rouge: LSU Press, 1996) 169.
31 New Orleans Parish Recorder, Marriage Records, Book 4, Folio 272.
32 Cheyenne County, Nebraska, County Court Records, Vol. 1. 169.
33 New Orleans Parish Board of Health, Death Records.
34 Edwards 1874 New Orleans Directory. 706.
35 Soard's 1875 New Orleans City Directory. 637.
36 Kimberly Hunger, *A Medley of Cultures & Politics in Reconstructed Louisiana* (New Orleans: Louisiana State Museum, 2004).
37 *New Orleans Times*, May 25, 1874.
38 City of New Orleans, 4th Municipal Police Court, Transcript, May 23, 1874.
39 *New Orleans Times*, May 25, 1874.
40 Police Court Transcript, May 25, 1874.
41 Ibid.
42 *New Orleans Republican*, November 14, 1875.
43 *New Orleans Republican*, November 25, 1875.
44 State of Louisiana, New Orleans Grand Jury Report, January 10, 1876.
45 Rousey, *Policing the Southern City*. 125, 170.
46 State of Louisiana, 1876 House Committee to Examine the Metropolitan Police, Transcript. 174.
47 Rousey, *Policing the Southern City*. 171.

CHAPTER 4

48 Wolfe's 1876-77 Omaha Directory. 188.
49 Public Broadcasting System, "Panic of 1873," *American Experience*, http:/ i /pbs.orgwbgh/amex/grant/peopleevents/e_panic.html

50 Frank Prassel, *The Western Peace Officer* (Norman: University of Oklahoma Press, 1972), 139.
51 Harold Hutton, *Doc Middleton: Life and Legends of the Notorious Plains Outlaw* (Chicago: Swallow Press, 1974), 254.
52 Cheyenne, Wyoming, City Council Minutes, February 12, 1878.
53 *Cheyenne Daily Leader*, February 28 and November 12, 1879
54 Hutton, *Doc Middleton*, 68.
55 *Sidney Telegraph*, May 3, 1879.
56 Rob Rybolt, "Whispering Smith," *Nebraskaland* (November, 1986), 37.
57 Hutton, *Doc Middleton*. 244.
58 "Doc Middleton, Road Agent and Bandit." *American History Network*. http://www.rootsweb.com/~wyoming/middleton_t.htm
59 Hutton, *Doc Middleton*. 143.
60 *Sidney Telegraph*, June 21, 1879.
61 Julia B. McGillycuddy, *McGillycuddy Agent* (Stanford: Stanford University Press, 1941), 128, 254.
62 Clark Fuller, *Pioneer Paths* (Broken Bow, Nebraska: Percell, 1974), 70.
63 McGillycuddy, *McGillycuddy Agent*, 128-130.
64 Ibid.
65 *Rapid City Black Hills Journal*, July 5, 1879.
66 Ibid.
67 Jesse Brown and A. M. Willard, *The Black Hills Trails* (New York: Arno Press, 1924), 300.
68 R. T. Lawton, "Necktie Party Ended Lame Johnny's Outlaw Career," *Deadwood Magazine*, http://deadwoodmagazine.com
69 *Sidney Telegraph*, July 12, 1879.
70 *Cheyenne Daily Leader*, November 5, 1878.
71 Kennett Harris, "Hawkbill," *The Teepee Book*, Vol. 1, No. 10, November-December, 1915. 10.
72 Brown, The Black Hills Trails. 275.
73 *Cheyenne Daily Leader*, November 12, 1879.
74 Clark Fuller, *Pioneer Paths*, 70.
75 Wayne C. Lee, *Wild Towns of Nebraska*, (Caldwell. Idaho: Caxton Press, 1992), 89.

76 Ibid., 91.
77 Grant L. Shumway, *History of Western Nebraska and its People* Lincoln: Western Publications, 1921), 153.
78 Ibid.
79 *Sidney Telegraph*, May 29, 1880.
80 Shumway, *History of Western Nebraska*, 153.
81 *Sidney Telegraph*, January 8, 1881.
82 Nellie Snyder Yost, *The Call of the Range* (Denver: Sage Books, 1966), 66.
83 Shumway, *History of Western Nebraska*, 154.
84 Doug Engebretson, *Empty Saddles, Forgotten Names* (Aberdeen, South Dakota: North Plains Press, 1982), 99-103.
85 *Cheyenne Daily Leader*, April 5, 1881.
86 Ibid.
87 William Kratville, Union Pacific Historian, e-mail to author, June 19. 2003.
88 U. S. Census, 1900, Idaho, Ada, Bosie, Ward 2, ED 4.
89 Ibid., ED 32.
90 Clark Fuller, *Pioneer Paths*, 75.
91 *Bozeman Avant Courier*, March 1, 1883.
92 Hutton, *Doc Middleton*, 175, 211.
93 *Sidney Telegraph*, August 3, 1878.
94 *Wyoming Lusk Herald*, "Employees of the Stage Line," May 14, 2003.

CHAPTER 5

95 C. L. Sonnichson, *The Mescalero Apaches* (Norman: University of Oklahoma Press, 1958), 211.
96 William H. Llewellyn, letter to the Commissioner of Indian Affairs, 1881.
97 National Archives and Records Administration, Bureau of Indian Affairs, Record Group 75, Entry 978, Roster of Agency Employees, 1853-1909, Vol, 11, 54.
98 "Kas-Tzidens Fury – Nana's Raid," Burch Media, http;//www.southernnewmexico.com (accessed January 10, 2003).

99 U. S. Government Printing Office, Commissioner of Indian Affairs Annual Report, 1881. 16.
100 William T. Hagen, *Indian Police and Judges* Lincoln: University of Nebraska Press, 1966), 80.
101 *Las Cruces Rio Grande Republican*, September 16 and 25, 1882.
102 Kennett Harris, "Hawkbill," *The Teepee Book*, (November-December, 1915), 7-10.
103 Mary Francis Morrow, National Archives and Records Administration, letter to the author, March 13, 2003.
104 Edgar Beecher Bronson, *The Red Blooded Heroes of the Frontier* (New York: George Doran Co., 1910), 84.
105 Harold Hutton, *Doc Middleton, Life and Legends of the Notorious Outlaw* (Chicago: Swallow Press, 1974), 261.
106 Anne DeCorey, "Edgar Bronson, Nebraska's Ranchman," *Nebraska History*, Vol. 81, No. 3, (Fall 2000), 112.
107 W. Llewellyn, Letter to the Secretary of the Interior, Office of Indian Affairs Correspondence, 1873-1900, February 13, 1883.
108 Slim Kohler, "The Indian Police Remingtons," *The Gun Report*, Vol. 38, No. 7 (November, 1992).
109 Leon Metz, *The Encyclopedia of Lawmen, Outlaws and Gunfighters* (New York: Checkmark, 2002).
110 Wilford E. Roeder, "Colonel William H. Llewellyn," www.thespanishamericanwarcentennial.com
111 *El Paso Daily Times*, February 21, 1894.

CHAPTER 6

112 Cheyenne, Wyoming, City Directory, 1884. 82.
113 Frank R. Prassel, *The Western Peace* Officer (Norman: University of Oklahoma Press, 1972), 144.
114 Larry K. Brown, *The Hog Ranches of Wyoming* (Glendo, Wyoming: High Plains Press, 1995), 15-17, 144-145.
115 William MacLeod Raine, *Guns of the* Frontier (Cambridge: Houghton Mifflin Co., 1940), 204.
116 Helena Huntington Smith, *The War on Powder* River (Lincoln: University of Nebraska Press, 1966), 185-186.

117 Prassel, *Western Peace Officer*, 148-149.
118 James W. Hewitt, "A Bad Day on the River," *The Nebraska Lawyer*, (March, 1999): 19-20.
119 Ibid.
120 James L. Smith, letter to Thomas B. Adams, Wyoming Stock Growers Association, May 26, 1886.
121 Murray L. Carroll, "Whispering Smith's Hundred Dollar Hit," *Quarterly of the National Association for Outlaw and Lawman History*, Vol. XXI, No. 1, (Summer, 1987).
122 Larry Kummer, Jackson Hole Historical Society, letter to the author, December 14, 2004.
123 Grant L. Shumway, *History of Western Nebraska and its People* (Lincoln: Western Publications, 1921), 153.
124 Nellie Snyder Yost, *The Call of the Range* (Denver: Sage Books, 1966), 144.
125 Ibid., 225.
126 Murray L. Carroll, letter to the author, November 10, 2004.
127 *Miles City, Montana, Daily Yellowstone Journal*, June 7, 1887.
128 Lorman L. Hoopes, "This Last West," *Historical Biography of Montana, 1876-1886*. 323.

CHAPTER 7

129 Utah Division of Corporations, Index Numbers 509 and 4327.
130 *Ogden Standard*, January 30, 1889.
131 Ibid., March 2, 1889.
132 Territory of Utah, County of Salt Lake, Third District Court, Case 551, November 4, 1889.
133 Ibid.
134 *Ogden Standard*, October 7, 1890.
135 Utah State Archives, Mercur Mining Records, Agency History No. 3193.
136 *Price Eastern Utah Advocate*, September 17, 1914.
137 *Price Eastern Utah Advocate*, February 5, 1891.
138 Ibid., February 5, 1891.
139 Frank R. Prassel, *The Western Peace Officer* (Norman: University of Oklahoma Press, 1972), 139.

140 Pearl Baker, *The Wild Bunch at Robber's Roost* (New York: Abelord-Schuman, 1971), 48.
141 Ibid., 47.
142 Charles Kelly, *The Outlaw Trail* (New York: Devin-Adair Co., 1959), 133.
143 Ibid., 135.
144 Jay Robert Nash, *Encyclopedia of Western Lawmen and Outlaws* (New York: DaCapo Press, 1992), 67.
145 Kelly, *The Outlaw Trail*, 134.
146 Nash, *Encyclopedia*, 310.
147 Kelly, *The Outlaw Trail*, 136.
148 Ibid., 138.
149 Western Mining and Railroad Museum Archives, Pleasant Valley Coal Company, Internal Correspondence, April 30, 1897.
150 Ibid., May 4, 1897.
151 Ibid., June 21, 1897.
152 *Price Eastern Utah* Advocate, May 12, 1904.
153 *Denver Post*, August 27, 1914.
154 Will Carver, Donna Ernst, Richard Patterson and Dan Buck, correspondence with the author. December, 2003.
155 *Price Eastern Utah Advocate*, December 12, 1904.
156 Ibid., June 18, 1908
157 Ibid., October 7, 1897.
158 Ibid., January 6, 1898.
159 Ibid.
160 Carbon County, Utah, Seventh Judicial District Court, Case 14.
161 Price Eastern Utah Advocate, August 18, 1898.
162 U. S. Census, 1900, Utah, Salt Lake, ED 65, Sheet 8.

CHAPTER 8

163 Robert K. DeArment, "Bat Masterson and the Boxing Club War of Denver," *Colorado Heritage* (Autumn, 2000): 30-31.
164 Ibid., 34.
165 Ibid.
166 Ibid.
167 Ibid., 34, 35.

168 *Denver Times*, February 7, 1905.
169 Ballenger and Richards, *1901 Denver City Directory*. 1269.
170 DeArment, "Bat Masterson," 35.
171 Various Denver directories list roomers who may have been James L. Smith in the Larimer and Curtis Street area intermittently from 1900 to 1914.
172 James D. Horan, *The Authentic Wild* West (New York: Crown Publishers, 1980), 59.
173 William MacLeod Raine, *Guns of the Frontier* (Cambridge: Houghton Mifflin Company, 1940), 255.
174 Paul O'Neil, *The End and the Myth* (Alexandria, Virginia: Time Life Books, 1979), 85.
175 *Sidney Telegraph*, May 9, 1903.
176 David J. Krajick, "Nerves of Steel," http:www.inlineofduty.com
177 Patrick Crowe, *Spreading Evil* (New York: Branwell Company, 1927).
178 U. S. Census, 1910, Colorado, Chaffee County, Institutions.
179 June Shaputis, "Mt. Olive Cemetery Prisoner Burials," U. S. GenWeb Project (1987) http:/www.rootsweb.com/co/cofiles.htm
180 *Leadville Herald Democrat*, July 21, 1912.
181 Ibid.
182 Shaputis, "Prisoner Burials".
183 *Leadville Herald Democrat*, July 20, 1912.

CHAPTER 9

184 *Denver Rocky Mountain News*, August 27, 1914.
185 Ibid., August 28, 1914.
186 Charles Kelly, *The Outlaw Trail* (New York: Devin-Adair Co., 1959), 136.
187 Family Search, International Genealogical Index v5.0, North America, www,family-search.org
188 Polk City Directory, 1900, Salt Lake City, Utah.
189 Sue Ann Martell, Western Mining & Railroad Museum, e-mail to the author, July 2, 2003.
190 *Denver Rocky Mountain News*, August 27, 1914.

191 M. Dougall, Riverside Cemetery, correspondence with the author, June 19, 2003.
192 *Denver Rocky Mountain News*, August 27, 1914.
193 *Denver* Post, August 27, 1914.
194 *Price Eastern Utah Advocate*, September 17, 1914.

ADDENDUM

195 Julia McGillycuddy, *McGillycuddy Agent* (Stanford: Stanford University Press, 1941), 128.
196 Grant L. Shumway, *History of Western Nebraska and its People* (Lincoln: Western Publications, 1921), 153.
197 Agnes Wright Spring, *The Cheyenne and Black Hills Stage and Express Routes* (Glendale: Arthur Clark Co., 1949).
198 Doug Engebretson, *Empty Saddles, Forgotten Names* (Aberdeen, WY: North Plains Press, 1982), 97.
199 Kennett Harris, "Hawkbill," *The Teepee Book*, Vol. 1, No. 10 (November-December, 1915): 6.
200 Edgar Beecher Bronson, *The Red Blooded Heroes of the Frontier*, (New York: George Doran Co, 1910) 78.
201 *Denver Times*, February 7, 1905.
202 Bronson, *The Red Blooded*, 78.
203 Shumway, *History of Western Nebraska*, 153.
204 McGillycuddy, *McGillycuddy Agent*, 128.
205 Bronson, *The Red Blooded*, 78.
206 *Sidney Telegraph*, May 29, 1880.
207 Bronson, *The Red Blooded*, 78.
208 Harris, *Hawkbill*, 11.
209 Beverly Linet, *Ladd- The Life, Legend and Legacy of Alan Ladd* (New York: Arbor House, 1979), 251.
210 Ibid., 249.
211 Ibid., 259-261.

BIBLIOGRAPHY

Baker, Pearl, *The Wild Bunch at Robber's Roost*, New York: Abelard-Schuman, 1971.

Ballenger and Richards, 1901 Denver City Directory.

Barefield, Jack, "Whispering Smith Rides Again," *The Railroadiana Express*, (Spring 1971).

Bronson, Edgar Beecher, *The Red Blooded Heroes of the Frontier*, New York: George H. Doran Co., 1910.

Brown, Jesse and A. M. Willard, *The Black Hills Trail*, New York: Arno Press, 1924.

Brown, Larry K., *The Hog Ranches of Wyoming*, Glendo (WY): High Plains Press, 1995.

Carbon County, Utah, Seventh Judicial District Court, Case 14, December 31, 1897.

Carroll, Murray L., "Whispering Smith's Hundred Dollar Hit," *Quarterly of the National Association and Center for Outlaw and Lawman History*, Vol. XII, No.1, (Summer 1987).

Cheyenne County, Nebraska, Historical Association, Research team. http://www.sidney-nebraska.com

Cheyenne County, Nebraska, Court Records, Vol. 1.

Cheyenne, Wyoming, City Council Minutes, February 12, 1878.

Cheyenne, Wyoming, City Directory, 1884.

City of New Orleans, Transcript, 4th Municipal Police Court, Case 841, November 13, 1875.

Civil War, Records of Volunteer Officers, National Archives & Records Administration, Vol. B.

Coleman, J. Winston, Jr., *Famous Kentucky Duels*, Lexington: Clay Press, 1969.

Crowe, Patrick, *Spreading Evil*, New York: Branwell Co., 1927.

DeArment, Robert K., "Bat Masterson and the Boxing Club of Denver," *Colorado Heritage*, (Autumn, 2000)

DeCorey, Anne, "Edgar Bronson, Nebraska's Ranchman," *Nebraska History*, Vol. 81, No. 3 (Fall 2000).

Devol, George H., *Forty Years as a Gambler on the Mississippi*, New York: Johnson Reprint Corp., 1892.

"Doc Middleton – Road Agent and Bandit," American History Network, www.rootsweb.com.

Dorsett, Lyle W., *The Queen City: A History of Denver*, Boulder: Pruett Publishing Co., 1973.

Edwards 1874 New Orleans Directory.

Engebretson, Doug, *Empty Saddles, Forgotten Names*, Aberdeen (SD): North Plains Press, 1982.

Everly, Elane C., "Freedmen's Bureau Records: An Overview,"

Family Search, International Genealogical Index, v.50, North America, www.family-search.org.

Fuller, Clark, *Pioneer Paths*, (Broken Bow (NE): Purcell Publishers, 1974).

Hagan, William T., *Indian Police and Judges*, Lincoln: University of Nebraska Press, 1966.

Harris, Kennett, "Hawkbill," *The Teepee Book*, Vol. I, No. 10 (November-December, 1915).

Hewitt, James W., "A Bad Day on the River," *The Nebraska Lawyer*, (March, 1999).

Hoopes, Lorman L., "This Last West," *Historical Biography of Montana-1876-1886*, Helena (MT): Falcon Press, 1990.

Horan, James D., *The Authentic Wild West*, New York: Crown Publishers, 1980.

Hunger, Kimberly, *A Medley of Cultures: Politics in Reconstructed Louisiana*, New Orleans: Louisiana State Museum, 2004.

Hutton, Harold, *Doc Middleton: Life and Legends of the Notorious Plains Outlaw*, Chicago: Swallow Press, 1974.

"Kas-Tzidens Fury – Nana's Raid," Burch Media, www.outhernew-mexico.com

Kelly, Charles, *The Outlaw Trail*, New York: Devin-Adair Co., 1959.

Kohler, Slim, "The Indian Police Remingtons," *The Gun Report*, Vol. 38, No. 7 (November, 1992).

Krajich, David J., "Nerves of Steel," www.inthelineofduty.com

Kunitz, Stanley J. and Howard Haycraft, *Twentieth Century Authors*, New York: H. W. Wilson Co., 1942.

Lawton, R. T., "Necktie Party Ended Lame Johnny's Outlaw Career," *Deadwood Magazine*, www.deadwoodmagazine.com.

Lee, Wayne C., *Wild Towns of Nebraska*, Caldwell (ID): Claxton Press, 1992.

Linet, Beverly, *Ladd- The Life, Legend and Legacy of Alan Ladd*, New York: Arbor House, 1979.

Maryland State Archives, Anne Arundel County Court, Marriage Licenses, CR 49, 158-2, MSA No. CM

McGillycuddy, Julia B., *McGillycuddy Agent*, Stanford: Stanford University Press, 1941.

Metz, Leon, *The Encyclopedia of Lawmen, outlaws and Gunfighters*, New York: Checkmark Press, 2002.

Nash, Jay Robert, *Encyclopedia of Western Lawman & Outlaws*, New York: DeCapo Press, 1992).

National Archives & Records Administration, Bureau of Indian Affairs Record Group 75, Entr 978, Roster of Agency Employees, 1853-1909, Vol. II.

New Orleans Parish Board of Health Death Records.

New Orleans Parish Recorder, Marriage Records, Folio 272, Book 4.

Nieman, Donald G., *To Set the Law in Motion: The Freedmen's Bureau and the Rights of Blacks, 1865-1868*, New York: KTO Press, 1979.

Official Records of the Union and Confederate Navies in the War of the Rebellion, Vol. 25, United States Naval Records Office.

O'Neil, Paul O., *The End and the Myth*, Alexandria: Time Life Books, 1979.

Polk City Directory, 1900, Salt Lake City, Farmer District, Institutions.

Prassel, Frank Richard, *The Western Peace Officer*, Norman: University of Oklahoma Press, 1972.

Public Broadcasting System, "Panic of 1873," American Experience, www.pbs.org

Raine, William MacLeod, *Guns of the Frontier*, Cambridge: Houghton Mifflin, 1940.

Reidy, Joseph P., "Black Men in Navy Blue During the Civil War," Quarterly of the National Archives and Records Administration, Vol. 33, No. 3, Fall 2001.

Roeder, Wilford E., "Colonel William H. H. Llewellyn," *The Spanish*

American War Centenial Website, www.spanishamericanwar.com.

Roster of Civilians Employed as Assistants, Agents and Inspectors by Thomas W. Conway, Assistant Commissioner, Bureau of Refugees, Freedmen and Abandoned Lands, State of Louisiana, National Archives Microfilm M1027, Roll 34.

Rousey, Dennis C., *Policing the Southern City: New Orleans, 1805-1889*, Baton Rouge: LSU Press, 1996.

Rybolt, Bob, "Whispering Smith," *Nebraskaland*, (November, 1986).

Shaputis, June, "Mt. Olivet Cemetery Prisoner Burials," U.S. GenWeb Project www.rootsweb.com.

Shumway, Grant L., *History of Western Nebraska and its People*, Lincoln: Western Publications, 1921.

Smith, Helena Huntington, *The War on Powder River*, Lincoln: University of Nebraska Press, 1966.

Soards' 1875 New Orleans Directory.

Sonnichen, C. L., *The Mescalero Apaches*, Norman: University of Oklahoma Press, 1958.

Spearman, Frank H., *Whispering Smith*, New York: Grosset & Dunlap, 1906.

State of Louisiana, New Orleans Superior Court, Grand Jury Report, January 10, 1886.

State of Louisiana, 1876 House Committee to Examine the Metropolitan Police, Transcript.

Territory of Utah, County of Salt Lake, 3rd District Court Record, Case 551, November 4, 1889.

Thomas, Samuel, Brigadier General, Headquarters, Bureau of Refugees, Freedmen and Abandoned Lands, State of Louisiana, Correspondence, March 9, 1867.

U. S. Census, 1840, Maryland, Anne Arundel County, District 1.

___. 1850, Delaware, New Castle County, Wilmington.

___. 1860, Maryland, Baltimore City, 1st Ward.

___. 1860, Ohio, Hamilton County, Cincinnati, Ward 4.

___. 1870, Maryland, Baltimore City, 12th Ward.

___. 1880, Wyoming, Cheyenne County.

___. 1900, Idaho, Ada County, Boise, Ward 2, ED 4, ED 32.

___. 1900, Utah, Salt Lake, ED 65.

___. 1900, Utah, Salt Lake, Farmer Precinct.

___. 1910, Colorado, Chaffee County, Buena Vista, Institutions.

U. S. Government Printing Office, Commissioner of Indian Affairs, Annual report, 1881.

Utah Division of Corporations, Index Number 509, 4327.

Utah State Archives, Agency History Number 3193, Mercer Mining District.

Western Mining and Railroad Museum, Helper, Utah, Pleasant Valley Coal Company Correspondence.

White, Howard A., The Freedmen's Bureau in Louisiana, Baton Rouge: LSU Press, 1970.

Wolfe's 1876-77 Omaha, Nebraska, Directory

Wright, Spring Agnes, *The Cheyenne and Black Hills Stage and Express Route,* Glendale: Arthur Clark Co, 1949.

Yost, Nellie Snyder, *The Call of the Range,* Denver: Sage Books, 1966.

INDEX

Alexander, Munson, 18, 39-43, 153
Allen, Chester K., 62-66
Allred, Charles W., 121, 122
Anne Arundel County, Maryland, 20

Bagley, Captain Frank, 32
Baltimore, Maryland, 21
Black Hills, 49, 52, 54, 61
Bonfils, Fred, 125-127
Boswell, N. K., 48
Boyle, Larry, 25, 142, 154
Braffett, M. P., 121, 122, 153
Branigan, Thomas, 80, 83
Bronson, Edgar Beecher, 80, 81, 150
Brown, Jesse, 55-59, 62, 73
Buena Vista Reformatory, 131, 133, 137
Buffalo Bill (William F. Cody), 128
Buffalo Gap, 56, 57

Caffey, Dr. William P., 139
Caffey, Frank (Benjamin F. Caffey) 114-119, 138, 139
Cairo, Illinois, 26
Calahan, Jim, 130
Canton, Frank, 93
Carpio, 79, 153
Cassidy, Butch (Robert LeRoy Parker), 112-115, 120, 139

Castle Gate, Utah, 107, 113-115, 146

Chadron, Nebraska, 86, 89, 118, 119
Chesney, James (Whitcomb Jim), 89
Cheyenne, Wyoming, 47, 48, 52, 54, 60, 61, 85, 98
Crawford, Captain Emmet, 56
Crowe, Patrick, 130, 131
Cudahy, Edward A., 129, 130

Davis, Ross, 55, 62, 65
Davis, Scott, 62, 65, 71, 73, 88
Deadwood City, 54, 56, 61
Denver & Rio Grande Railroad, 97-99, 108, 113, 116, 117, 119, 123, 135
Denver, Colorado, 118, 124-127, 134-136
Devereaux, Thomas, 17, 36, 40-44
Donant, Gus, 110, 115, 121

Eisley, George, 48

Flannagan, Dennis, 63-67, 70, 102, 152
Floto, Otto C., 125
Foote, John W., 138
Fort Hartstuff, 51
Fort Laramie, 59
Fort Meade, 60
Fort Robinson, 56, 86
Fort Sheridan, 55
Fort Stanton, 79
Feedmen's Bureau, 24, 31-33, 38, 61

Garrett, Pat, 75, 154
Give-Me-A-Horse, 79, 153
Grimes, Lou (Curley), 60

Hamlin, John J., 90, 91
Harris, Frank, 56, 58, 69
Hazen, Lyman, 51
Hill, Gale, 55, 62, 73
Hog Ranches, 88
Horn, Tom, 88
Hughes, Sheriff Robert

Jackson, William C. (Teton Jackson), 93
Johnson County War, 88

Kramer, George W., 118
Keliher, Timothy T., 13, 14

Ladd, Alan, 16, 154, 155
Lame Johnny (Donahue, Cornelius), 54-60, 69, 76, 153
Lay, Elzy, 114. 115, 118, 120, 139
Leach, M. E., 48
Leadville, Colorado, 131-133, 136
LeFors, Joe, 13, 14
Llewellyn, William H., 51-54, 60, 76, 78-83
Longabaugh, Harry (Sundance Kid), 95
Lykens, William, 51, 52

McCarty, Cornelius, 63-66, 69, 71
McDonald, John, 69, 70, 76, 153
McGillycuddy, Dr. Valentine, 53-55, 58
McIntosh, John T., 98, 100, 101, 106

McLaughlin, Archie, 59, 153

Mannion, Anna, 36. See also Smith, Anna
Mansfield, Billy, 59, 153
Marko, Stephen, 132-136, 153
Marshall, Jim, 128
Masterson, Bat, 124-128
Maxwell, C. L. (Gunplay), 109, 112, 114, 117, 119, 120, 138
May, Boone, 55, 60, 62
May, Jim, 55, 59
Meeks, Bob, 114, 120
Meeks, Joe, 114, 115
Mescalero Indian Reservation, 76
Mickey, Governor, 129-131
Middlemiss, John R., 98-107
Middleton, Doc, 49-54, 60, 72, 76, 81
Miles, George A., 92
Mills, J. G., 48, 49, 60, 61, 102

Nana, 76, 78
Nantizli, 79
New Orleans Metropolitan Police 33-35, 38, 44
Northern Pacific Railway, 95, 100, 108

Ogden, Utah, 98
Omaha, Nebraska, 46

Parrott, George (Big Nose George), 59
Perry, Lydia, 19-21
Peso, Captain, 77, 80
Pine Ridge Indian Reservation, 53, 54, 56, 148

Pleasant Valley Coal Company, 107, 109, 113, 116, 119, 123, 139, 148
Price, Utah, 112

Reed, Charley, 50
Rideout, D. O., 101, 102
Riverside Cemetery, 140
Robinson, Robert, 98
Ryan, Thomas, 64, 71

Sample, Billy, 73
Shores, Cyrus, 116-119, 123
Sidney, Nebraska, 37, 49-51, 54, 55, 61, 63, 67, 69, 102, 128
Smith, Anna, 36, 37, 47, 66, 76, 85, 131, 151. See also Mannion, Anna
Smith, Eugene, 73
Smith James, 19
Smith, James B., 84
Smith, James H., 22

Smith, James L. (Whispering Smith)
  early life, 19-23
  military service, 24-28
  plantation inspector, 32, 33
  New Orleans detective, 34-43
  Union Pacific detective, 48-71
  Indian reservation police chief, 76-82
  stock inspector, 85-95
  private detective, 99-106
  security officer, 109-123
  prison guard, 131-136
  death, 139-146

Smith, Johnny (Morrell, J. H.), 90-92
Smith Joseph (genealogy), 20, 21
Smith, Joseph (outlaw), 50
Smith, Wilson B., 95
Spearman, Frank H., 13-16
Sturgis, Tom, 94
Swan, Alexander H., 98, 100
Swan, William R. 98, 106

Tammen, Harry, 125-128
Thurston, John, 63-66, 148

Union Pacific Railway, 46-52, 62, 64, 71, 108, 142

Valentine, Nebraska, 90
VanDyke, William, 98-100

Wade, Albert (Kid Wade), 89
Walker, Joe, 114, 115, 120
Walters, Patsy, 63-66, 69, 70, 72, 153
Warf, J. W., 112, 121, 122, 153
Williams, W. R., 95, 100, 101
Wilmington, Delaware, 22, 26
Wyoming Cattle Growers Association, 81, 85, 86, 90-98, 100, 129

www.ingramcontent.com/pod-product-compliance
Lightning Source LLC
Chambersburg PA
CBHW032258150426
43195CB00008BA/497